Choosing Children's Books

David Booth
Larry Swartz
Meguido Zola

Pembroke Publishers Limited

We wish to record our thanks to the following:

Vancouver Kids Books
The Children's Book Store
Reading, Inc.

and to

The Librarians (in schools, in communities, in universities)
who helped us to make our choices.

Copyright © 1987 Pembroke Publishers Limited
528 Hood Road
Markham, Ontario L3R 3K9

Canadian Cataloguing in Publication Data

Booth, David
  Choosing children's books

Includes index.
ISBN 0-921217-12-9

1. Children's literature – Bibliography.
2. Bibliography – Best books – Children's literature.
3. Children – Books and reading. I. Swartz, Larry.
II. Zola, Meguido, 1939- . III. Title.

Z1037.B66 1987   011'.62   C87-094617-X

Editor: Nancy Christoffer
Type: Jay Tee Graphics Ltd.

Printed and bound in Canada
0 9 8 7 6 5 4 3 2 1

Table of Contents

Choosing Books for Children

There are tens of thousands of books for today's children—classics from the past, books made into films and television shows, award winners, comics, pop-up books, realistic novels, folk tales newly illustrated, poetry anthologies, and theme collections. The list is truly endless. The challenge is to choose wisely.

For some children, books are readily available—at home, in school, in libraries, at children's bookstores, and from mail-order houses. For others, books are scarce commodities, and individual needs may seldom be met.

For some children, meeting books as babies was an everyday occurrence, and sharing books with loving adults was always a happy experience. For others, school provided the only books they met, and these often took the shape of traditional school texts, with little or no allowance for individual needs and wants.

Most adults need help in bringing the appropriate book to children at the appropriate moment. We rely on knowledgeable teachers, librarians, critics, friends, children's choices, and recommended lists to build our own selections. There are many books about books on the market. As educators who work with teachers, parents, and children we are always building our own lists. These include books that work well in one-on-one situations, and with groups of children. Distinguishing between books children want to read, and books they can be encouraged to read is a delicate balance. We decided to bravely collate all of our experience, and to organize it for most effective use.

Putting together this type of book was a project full of difficulties:
- what would we include?
- what would we leave out?
- what would our selection criteria be?
- would our collection of books be a representative selection?
- would each entry have to have been read, or more importantly, have been used with children by one of us?
- would each entry have to have been read, or more important, have been used with children by one of us?
- would we choose children's favorites, critics' favorites, or our own favorites?

And so, we began: David Booth, a language arts professor at the University of Toronto; Larry Swartz, a resource teacher for the Peel Board of Education; and Meguido Zola, a professor of children's literature at Simon Fraser University.

We are each a devoted fan of children's books and use them in our work with teachers, parents, and children, with our families, and for our own pleasure. While each of us reads a wide range of formats, our individual interests gave us a focus for the structure of the book: Meguido Zola had a marvellous collection of books for very young children developed for his undergraduate and graduate seminars in Children's Literature and Early Childhood Education; David Booth had used his collection of picture books with all ages of children in reading aloud sessions and in educational drama experiences; Larry Swartz had amassed a great many novels for young people for use with both the children he taught and the adults in his in-service courses.

We wanted to recommend books to be read aloud to children of all ages—at home, at school, at camp, and at the library.

We wanted to help adults find a suitable book for a special child to read at a particular time, a book that would engage the youngster, pull the reader inside the print, and cause reading to be a meaning-making activity from the very beginning.

We wanted every child to meet books, freed from tension and failure, ready to challenge, appreciate, wonder, and laugh.

We wanted books to be the normal attributes of childhood, not icons to be revered or tasks to be completed.

Most of all, we wanted to share our own delight in experiencing these books and exploring them with children and adults.

So many favorites, so many treasures. How would we make them accessible to the readers of our book?

Taking our cue from Dorothy Butler's work *Babies Need Books*, we organized our selections into four very general categories:

1. Books for preschool children, 0 to 5
   Our choices for this division bleed into the next since children mature at different stages. The needs and interests of the child should outweigh all adult classification systems.
2. Books for primary children, 5 to 8
   This section includes the beginning reader, the developing reader, and the independent reader. It explores the common link of the children's need to be read aloud to, to read along with adults, and to read on their own, at whatever their reading level.
3. Books for middle readers, 8 to 11
   Youngsters at this age are at many different levels of abilities and interests. Common themes are one technique to assist in creating options for reading.

4. Books for young adolescents, 11 to 14
   Patterns of reading are now already established. Our aim is to
   remind those adults in charge of selecting and motivating of the
   wondrous variety of books available to these maturing readers.

We have included toy books, picture books, easy read books,
anthologies, collections, folktales, poems, readers, novels,
information books, classics, and books children love in spite of us.
Usually the selections are grouped under these genres, but
sometimes we suggest themes to encourage wide reading. We have
also listed books to be read aloud, including picture books for older
children.

We decided to arrange the lists in two ways:
- books generally read by adults to or with children would be
  arranged in alphabetical order
- books read by children on their own would be arranged by the
  level of difficulty of the material—a very rough measure, but
  perhaps appropriate in the beginning process of helping children
  meet books successfully.

Books are often available in both hardback and paperback editions.
We generally present the most recent publishing information. A
paperback book may be handled by different distributors in different
areas or at different times. Your library or bookstore can help you
locate the book that best fits your needs.

We have written the book for you as an adult entrusted with the
responsibility of bringing children and books together, and of
encouraging a warm relationship between the two. However, in the
end, this book is for the children who need our advice, wisdom,
support, and nurturing as they develop into independent readers
who not only *can* read, but *do* read.

Preschool Children

It is important to introduce young children to books as early as possible in their lives, and the earlier the better. One has only to watch a baby or young infant with a book, favorite or new, patting the pictures, pointing out familiar objects, exclaiming, laughing, babbling. Books are real and vivid experiences for children.

Psychologists tell us that the greatest part of our intellectual development takes place before the age of five, and another half of that again before the age of eight. The child's preschool years are therefore the most critical ones developmentally. It follows that this period of a child's life requires the richest of educational experiences.

A loving, enthusiastic introduction to the world of literature is, according to the most recent research, one of the most important elements of such an education. Books, in the words of teacher, bookseller, and writer Dorothy Butler, "can be bridges between children and parents, and children and the world." Books contribute significantly to the development of thinking and language in the preschool child. Books nurture learning, and they enhance children's understanding of self and their world. Books contribute to the development of young children's communication skills as well as encouraging positive relationships with those close to them. For parents and other caregivers this last point should be a compelling enough reason for sharing books with children.

Cloth Books

These are books that the youngest baby can taste but not tear, pull apart, or shred—that's why cloth or rag books, and their newer plasticized variants, were invented. But they do have their drawbacks. While most cloth books are indifferent in content and quality, some are nevertheless worth considering for the youngest baby. This sampling—soft, nontoxic, and washable—covers the range.

COUNTING
Dick Bruna
Dean's International Children's Books, 1974
Bruna illustrations, in the familiar square and simple format, are reproduced on cloth.
OTHER BOOKS: *Dressing; Eating; Working; All My Toys; At the Zoo; Here's Miffy; On the Farm.*

HELLO, BABY
Lin Howard
Platt & Munk, 1984
A machine-washable, percale, foam-stuffed pillow that unfolds to become a picture book printed in non-toxic colors.
OTHER BOOKS: *Baby Talk*

SPOT'S TOYS
Eric Hill
G.P. Putnam's Sons, 1984
The popular, lovable dog Spot is here pictured with his toys in his first vinyl book.
OTHER BOOKS: *Sweet Dreams, Spot*

TOYS
Andrew MacConville
Octopus, 1986
A half-dozen simple illustrations in a color-fast, washable, quality cloth book.
OTHER BOOKS: *Food; Indoors; Outdoors.*

Board Books

The last few years have seen a resurgence of the board book as well
as advances in its design. Board books are invariably of higher
artistic and literary merit than rag books; and, with their stout,
rounded, plastic-coated or laminated, washable pages, they will
outlast not only any rag book but the playpen as well. The books
presented here range from books that are about babies and infants to
those that feature older children; from books that deal with what
is simple, easy, and familiar to books that deal with what is more
complex and unfamiliar; from books that are essentially look-and-say
themed lists of people, animals, and objects, to books that explore
concepts and ideas, to books whose contents are linked together by
narrating a sequence of events or telling a story.

AT THE PLAYGROUND
Anne Rockwell
Thomas Y. Crowell, 1986
All about what toddler does at the playground, with simple
illustrations.
OTHER BOOKS: *At Night; In the Morning; In the Rain.*

BABY BEN'S NOISY BOOK
Harriet Ziefert; ill. Norman Gorbaty
Random House, 1984
The world of sights, sounds, and early learning concepts are
presented from a baby's viewpoint.
SEQUELS: *Baby Ben's Busy Book; Baby Ben's Bow-Wow Book; Baby Ben's
Go-Go Book.*

BATHTIME
photographed by Lars Wik
Methuen, 1975
These plastic-spiral bound board books show familiar everyday
activities in the life of a young toddler who could be either boy or
girl. Good for the very youngest child to point to and talk about.
OTHER BOOKS: *At Home; Bedtime; Mealtime; My Clothes; Play at Home;
Playing Together; Playtime.*

FIND THE TEDDY
Stephen Cartwright & Claudia Zeff
Usborne, 1983
These books give young children the challenge of naming familiar
objects, amusing situations to talk about, and things to look for.
SEQUELS: *Find the Bird; Find the Duck; Find the Kitten; Find the Piglet;
Find the Puppy.*

GUESS WHO?
Grahame Corbett
Walker, 1982
Peek-a-boo guessing games illustrate concepts of movement and change. For preschoolers and their parents to play together.
OTHER BOOKS: *What Number Now?; Who Is Hiding?; Who Is Next?; Who's Inside?; Watching; Hiding; Playing; Working.*

HERE'S BAABEE
Dayal Kaur Khalsa
Tundra Books, 1983
This stepped, three-part Canadian series features an infant of indeterminate age, sex, and race in everyday activities. These books are designed to be started with babies to help them recognize color, shape, etc. Beginning with fold-out friezes with holes through which to thread string for hanging over baby's crib, the series graduates to laminated board books.
SERIES I: *Baabee's Things; Baabee Gets Dressed; Baabee's Home.*
SERIES II: *Baabee Goes Out; Baabee Plays; Baabee Takes a Bath; Goodnight, Baabee.*
SERIES III: *Bon Voyage, Baabee; Happy Birthday, Baabee; Merry Christmas, Baabee; Welcome, Twins.*

I CAN
Helen Oxenbury
Walker, 1985
A baby's world is full of new delights, and in this book a toddler discovers some of them. Bright drawings in watercolors are the hallmark of this British artist.
OTHER BOOKS: *I Hear; I See; I Touch; All Fall Down; Clap Hands; Say Goodnight; Tickle, Tickle; Working; Dressing; Family; Friends; Playing; Monkey See, Monkey Do; Beach Day; Good Night; Good Morning; Mother's Helper; Shopping.*

I LIKE EATING . . .
Peter Currie
Heinemann, 1986
Illustrations on a long accordion-folding board book. The top of each page is cut out in the shape of the object represented.
OTHER BOOKS: *A Like Driving...; I Like Wearing....*

I'M FROG
Jan Pienkowski
Walker, 1987
Frog tells his story in large pictures of vibrant color.
SEQUELS: *I'm Cat; I'm Mouse; I'm Panda.*

LITTLE DOLLS
Rodney Peppe
Viking Kestrel, 1984
Little toys play a variety of imagination filled games in this book and
its sequels.
SEQUELS: *Little Circus; Little Games; Little Numbers; Little Wheels.*

MAX'S RIDE
Rosemary Wells
Dial Books, 1979
Max, a feisty and determined bunny, takes a wild ride in—and out
of—his carriage, to let his readers explore the concepts of over and
under and through. These stories will appeal to children of wide age
range while presenting concepts in terms that the youngest can
grasp.
OTHER BOOKS: *Max's First Word; Max's Toys; Max's New Suit; Max's
Bath; Max's Birthday; Max's Breakfast; Max's Bedtime.*

MY BEDTIME
Rod Campbell
Blackie & Son, 1985
A softly colored accordion-book featuring all of baby's favorite things
for bedtime. The top of this fold-out laminated board book is cut out
around the shape of each simple object represented.
OTHER BOOKS: *My Favourite Things; My Meals; My Toys.*

MY TOYS
Dick Bruna
Derrydale, 1986
An introduction, in an accordion-folding board book, to this artist
whose baby books are known and loved the world over.
OTHER BOOKS: *My Animals; My Garden; My Street; My Meals; Out and
About; Good Morning; Good Night.*

PLAYTHINGS
Simms Taback
Heinemann, 1986
A baby-fist sized board book comprising two dozen labelled

illustrations. Point to the picture and ask baby to say the word; say the word and ask baby to point to the picture; cover the picture and ask baby "What's hiding?" The permutations are endless.
OTHER BOOKS: *Food; Clothing.*

Toy Books: Pop-Ups, Lift-Downs, Fold-Outs

Some books invite—and require—an overt kind of participation. Such toy books or pop-up books or movable books, however they are variously called, usually require the reader to interact with the book in a physical way—turn it around, peep through a hole, look through a transparent overlay, lift a flap, pull back a tab, etc. These creations have enjoyed a great renaissance since the mid-1970's, and include some of the finest examples of the art of children's books.

ANIMALS FOR SALE
Bruno Munari
William Collins Sons, 1945
These picture books are simple but ingenious examples of the art of the paper engineer with a good story to tell.
OTHER BOOKS: *Jimmy Has Lost His Cap. Where Is It?; Circus in the Mist; Tic, Tac and Toc; The Birthday Present; The Elephant's Wish; Who's There? Open the Door.*

ANYBODY AT HOME?
H.A. Rey
Houghton Mifflin, 1942
Each picture holds a secret. Lift the flap and discover it in these tiny books by the creator of Curious George.
OTHER BOOKS: *Feed the Animals; See the Circus; Where's My Baby?*

BABY BEN GETS DRESSED
Harriet Ziefert; ill. Norman Gorbaty
Random House, 1985
This baby is a cheerful character who gets up to all kinds of things, and his young audiences will love him as they see what he's doing behind the page flaps.
OTHER BOOKS: *Suppertime for Baby Ben; Bear's Busy Morning; Bear All Year; Bear Gets Dressed; Bear Goes Shopping.*

BOO! WHO?: A LIFT THE FLAP BOOK
Colin and Jacqui Hawkins
Holt, Rinehart & Winston, 1983
Pictures on each page—a castle, window-shutters, a rabbit hutch—all
with flaps to open to see who is inside calling out "Boo!"
OTHER BOOKS: *What's the Time Mr. Wolf?*

CATCH THE BALL
Eric Carle
Philomel, 1982
An illustrated book whose cut-out shapes, movable parts, and board
pages engage the child in a game designed to teach number skills,
color and object identification, and manual dexterity.
OTHER BOOKS: *Let's Paint a Rainbow; What's For Lunch?; The Very
Hungry Caterpillar; A Very Long Tail; A Very Long Train; The Grouchy
Ladybug; The Mixed-Up Chameleon; The Secret Birthday Message; The
Honeybee and the Robber; Watch Out! A Giant.*

DOLLHOUSE
Harry Saffren; ill. Sheilah Beckett
Random House, 1981
An intricately detailed dollhouse springs from the pages, including
extra sheets of cut-out furniture, when the child opens this book flat.
OTHER BOOKS: *A Victorian Dollhouse*

IN MY GARDEN
Ron Maris
Julia MacRae Books, 1987
The youngest child can look behind each split page to find out, and
count, what is in the garden.
OTHER BOOKS: *Are You There, Bear?; Is Anyone At Home; My Book.*

LOOK INSIDE! ALL KINDS OF PLACES
Rod Campbell
Abelard-Schuman, 1983
A first lift-the-flap book for the very young where they can look
inside a fire-engine, a submarine, and a spaceship.
SEQUEL: *Look Inside! Land, Sea and Air*
OTHER BOOKS: *Magic Circus; Magic Fairground; From Gran; Big and
Strong; Cars and Trucks; Speed; Playwheels.*

WHAT'S MISSING?
R & A van der Meer
Watts, 1983
Thinking and observation games solved by opening the flaps on
laminated accordion-folding friezes.
OTHER BOOKS: *Where Is the Baby?; Where Is the Mouse?; Who Eats What?*

YUM YUM
Janet & Allen Ahlberg
Viking Kestrel, 1984
A toy book in which slots cut into every page hold different objects
that can be rearranged to make new combinations.
OTHER BOOKS: *Playmates*

Mother Goose

The musical quality of the rhymes' varied language patterns, as well
as the natural opportunity they offer for the child's active
participation in movement, game, and song are, in part, what have
given the nursery and Mother Goose rhymes their enduring appeal
over centuries. Just as vital, too, are the rhymes' rich narrative
qualities—they tell brief, action-packed, satisfying stories full of
humor and hyperbole. Lastly, in the words of American critic Eileen
Burke, these rhymes "have appealed strongly to children's artists
and have spurred a collective portfolio of children's . . . illustrations
unlike all others for richness and craftsmanship and imagination."
For these reasons, Mother Goose will amuse and enterain and
instruct in different ways throughout childhood. And she will lodge
deep in the memory.

ARNOLD LOBEL'S BOOK OF MOTHER GOOSE
compiled by Arnold Lobel
Random House, 1986
Illustrating three hundred selections from Mother Goose, Lobel calls
the verses a "lively, lusty body of literature" that has all too often
been given interpretations that are "so polite, so genteel, so well-
behaved. My concept of Mother Goose is just the opposite: bawdy
and naughty."
OTHER BOOKS: *Gregory Griggs and Other Nursery Rhyme People; Whiskers
and Rhymes.*

THE BABY'S LAP BOOK
Kay Chorao
E.P. Dutton Books, 1977
Softly sketched black and white drawings bordered in pastels set off fifty-eight nursery rhymes that are most often sung to infants. A comforting lap book.

THE BOOK OF NURSERY & MOTHER GOOSE RHYMES
Marguerite de Angeli
Doubleday, 1954
A large American collection of three hundred and seventy-six rhymes, including a few riddles, finger-plays, and word games. Illustrated with black and white old-fashioned drawings interspersed with colored plates.

BRIAN WILDSMITH'S MOTHER GOOSE
Brian Wildsmith
Oxford University Press, 1963
A one-rhyme-to-a-page collection that is notable for its illustrations.

FATHER FOX'S PENNYRHYMES
Clyde Watson
Scholastic, 1975
Rhythmic poems which use the patterns and idioms of traditional nursery rhymes.
OTHER BOOKS: *Catch Me & Kiss Me & Say It Again*

THE HELEN OXENBURY NURSERY RHYME BOOK
compiled by Brian Alderson; ill. Helen Oxenbury
Heinemann, 1986
A book based on the beloved *Cakes and Custard* by the same team.

LAVENDER'S BLUE
compiled by Kathleen Lines; ill. Harold Jones
Oxford University Press, 1954
A comprehensive collection distinguished by pictures of quiet dignity in alternate double-spreads of black and white and muted pastels.

MARGUERITE, GO WASH YOUR FEET
Wallace Tripp
Little, Brown & Company, 1985
These nonsense rhymes from Mother Goose are a treat for any child.
OTHER BOOKS: *Granfa' Grig Had a Pig & Other Rhymes Without Reason from Mother Goose; A Great Big Ugly Man Came Up & Tied His Horse to Me.*

MOTHER GOOSE COMES TO CABLE STREET
compiled by Rosemary Stones and Andrew Mann; ill. Dan Jones
Kestrel Books, 1977
An illustrated multi-ethnic Mother Goose—nursery rhymes in a modern urban settling, London's East End, where the boys and girls are of all races.

THE MOTHER GOOSE TREASURY
compiled by Raymond Briggs
Picture Puffins, 1978
A storehouse of rhymes crammed with humorous illustrations that will appeal to all ages. Jim Trelease calls this Kate Greenway Medal winner "the best collection of nursery rhymes to be had."

NICOLA BAILEY'S BOOK OF NURSERY RHYMES
compiled by Nicola Bailey
Picture Puffins, 1984
A score of favorite nursery rhymes are set off by miniature paintings in the Victorian style that are replete with detail.
OTHER BOOKS: *Bedtime & Moonshine*

THE OXFORD NURSERY RHYME BOOK
compiled by Iona and Peter Opie
Oxford University Press, 1955
A collection of over eight hundred rhymes illustrated with black and white woodcuts, to be used as a reference rather than for sharing with a child.
OTHER BOOKS: *A Nursery Companion*

QUENTIN BLAKE'S NURSERY RHYME BOOK
compiled by Quentin Blake
Picture Puffins, 1986
A collection of lesser known nursery rhymes complemented by the artist's cartoons.

Rhyme, Verse, Jingle and Song

Poetry is not irregular lines down the printed page but, in the words of Northrop Frye, "something very close to dance and song, something to walk down the street keeping time to." Poetry, with its shapes, patterns, and forms, its rhythms and rhymes, and its imagery, has been rightly called the music of language and literature.

Young children have a strong affinity for this music: poetry elicits the most acute and active listening, it engenders conversation, and it stimulates all kinds of often spontaneous participation through movement and game and play. Young children should be immersed in poetry and music. The following is but a representative sample available for baby and preschooler.

THE BABY'S GOOD MORNING BOOK
Kay Chorao
E.P. Dutton Books, 1986
An anthology of verse and song that is bright as a sunny day, with illustrations as cheerful as a morning hug.
OTHER BOOKS: *The Baby's Goodnight Book*

DAYS ARE WHERE WE LIVE & OTHER POEMS
compiled by Jill Bennett; ill. Maureen Roffey
Bodley Head, 1981
Twenty-four little poems arranged so as to roughly follow the patterns of a young child's day.
OTHER BOOKS: *Roger was a Razor Fish*

DON'T PUT MUSTARD IN THE CUSTARD
Michael Rosen; ill. Quentin Blake
Andre Deutsch, 1985
A collection of funny verse that is immediately accessible to the older toddler: Britain's best loved pop poet and most prolific cartoonist have remarkable insight into the ways of children and the meaning of poetry.
OTHER BOOKS: *You Can't Catch Me!*

THE ELEPHANT
Colin and Jacqui Hawkins
Viking Kestrel, 1985
An illustrated rhyming game, with instructions for the actions on the back cover and a surprise at the end—a pop-up page.
OTHER BOOKS: *Incy Wincy Spider; Round the Garden; This Little Pig.*

HAND RHYMES
Marc Brown
E.P. Dutton Books, 1985
Little hands will wiggle, point, and stretch as they learn to animate
these fourteen hand games. Color pictures are accompanied by easy-
to-follow diagrams detailing the hand movements.
OTHER BOOKS: *Finger Rhymes*

JELLY BELLY
Dennis Lee; ill. Juan Wijngaard
Macmillan, 1983
A collection of new—mostly nonsense—nursery rhymes by this
Canadian poet. With illustrations full of detail and color.
OTHER BOOKS: *Garbage Delight; Alligator Pie; Nicholas Knock & Other
Rhymes.*

ORANGES AND LEMONS
compiled by Karen King; ill. Ian Beck
Oxford University Press, 1985
A collection of twenty-two modern and traditional singing and
dancing games. Each game is accompanied by a large picture for
looking at, clearly illustrated instructions and tips for playing the
game, and music, including chords for the guitar.

ROUND AND ROUND THE GARDEN
compiled by Sarah Williams; ill. Ian Beck
Oxford University Press, 1983
An illustrated collection of forty traditional play rhymes with full-
color drawings to show exactly how to play Mousie, Five Fat Peas,
Knock At The Door, and others.
OTHER BOOKS: *Ride on Cock Horse: Knee Jogging Rhymes, Patting Songs
& Lullabies*

SALLY GO ROUND THE SUN
collected by Edith Fowke; ill. Carlos Marchion
McClelland & Stewart, 1969
A prize-winning Canadian collection of playroom, sandlot, and
street-corner jingle and song, rhyme and verse. This illustrated book
presents some three hundred singing games, clapping games and
songs, skipping and ball-bouncing rhymes, taunts, teases, and silly
songs.

SOLOMON GRUNDY
Susan Hoguet
E.P. Dutton Books, 1986
Hoguet expands the nursery rhyme from a week's passing to a lifetime that reflects 74 years of American history.

THERE WERE TEN IN THE BED
Pam Adams
Child's Play, 1979
An example of the profusion of individual songs for young children that exist in picture book format, this particular one in movable book form.

THIS LITTLE PIGGY
Shelagh McGee
Hutchinson Publishing Group, 1987
A rhyme and a game to share with baby. Attractively illustrated, with instructions.
OTHER BOOKS: *One Two Buckle My Shoe; Round and Round; Two Little Dicky Birds.*

Picture Books/Theme Books

Unlike the illustrated book, where pictures serve as mere illumination and extension of some aspect of the text, the picture book is one in which text, where there is one, and illustrations are of equal importance, and are integrated. In this sense, as the critic Selma Lanes has pointed out, the picture book "bears resemblance to Siamese twins: the words cannot stand independent of the illustrations nor, in theory at least, can the pictures without text. Separately, their contribution is thin, incomplete. Together, they comprise a fully satisfying experience."

Picture books are the staple book for young children, and have been so for a long time. For, as the seventeenth century writer Comenius wrote in his *Orbis Sensualium Pictus*, published in Nuremberg in 1658, and the first known children's picture book, "Pictures are the most intelligible books children can look upon."

Wordless Books

Wordless books are picture books in which the story is told entirely through pictures. Possessing features in common with television and comics, wordless books are popular with children of all ages. They are also useful in preparing children for reading. They predispose young children to an attitude toward books as a source of pleasure; they develop reading readiness, for instance, through handling a book, turning the pages, following sequence left to right; and they develop interpretation of and response to the story told by the pictures.

THE ADVENTURES OF PADDY PORK
John S. Goodall
Macmillan, 1968
One of a series of wordless books about the misadventures of a naughty pig with bottomless curiosity. A more sophisticated series than most for the pre-schooler.
OTHER BOOKS: *Creepy Castle; Jacko; Kelly; Dot and Esmerelda; Naughty Nancy the Bad Bridesmaid; Paddy Finds a Job; Paddy Goes Travelling; Paddy Pork — Odd Jobs; Paddy Pork's Holiday; Paddy's New Hat; Paddy's Evening Out; Paddy Under Water; Shrewbettina Goes to Work; Shrewbettina's Birthday; The Midnight Adventures of Kelly, Dot and Esmerelda; The Ballooning Adventures of Paddy Pork; The Surprise Picnic.*

A BOY, A DOG AND A FROG
Mercer Mayer
Dial Books, 1967
A boy and a dog have a hard time catching a frog. This small-format book and its sequels are examples of the art of wordless cartooning.
SEQUELS: *Frog, Where Are You?; A Boy, A Dog, A Frog, and A Friend; Frog Goes to Dinner; One Frog Too Many.*
OTHER BOOKS: *Ah Choo!; Hiccup.*

CATCH THAT CAT!
Fernando Krahn
E.P. Dutton Books, 1978
The exotic trouble a little boy gets into trying to catch his runaway cat. Black and white illustrations tell the story.
OTHER BOOKS: *A Flying Saucer Full of Spaghetti; Here Comes Alex Pumpernickel; The Great Ape; The Mystery of the Giant Footprints; Who's Seen the Scissors?*

CHANGES, CHANGES
Pat Hutchins
Bodley Head, 1970
An easily read sequence in which two wooden dolls create for themselves, out of play blocks, a house, a fire-engine, a boat, a truck, etc. as their adventure calls for these objects.

DO YOU WANT TO BE MY FRIEND?
Eric Carle
Thomas Y. Crowell, 1971
A cleverly designed book that encourages the beginning reader to turn each page as the mouse, approaching the tail of one animal after another asks: "Do you want to be my friend?"

RAIN
Peter Spier
William Collins Sons, 1982
The story of what a brother and sister do through a rainy day and night, both indoors and out of doors. Children will love these pages of pen-sketched watercolors.
OTHER BOOKS: *Bored—Nothing To Do!; Christmas; Noah's Ark.*

A STORY TO TELL
Dick Bruna
Methuen, 1968
A story to tell from the simplest of these classic illustrations.
OTHER BOOKS: *Another Story to Tell*

SUNSHINE
Jan Ormerod
Viking Kestrel, 1981
For the very youngest, a wordless book that chronicles through the eyes of a little girl the first hour of a family day. The humorous drawings in watercolors won the illustrator Britain's Mother Goose Award.
OTHER BOOKS: *Moonlight*

UP AND UP
Shirley Hughes
Bodley Head, 1979
A young girl magically realizes her dream of flying. A fine example of the cartoonist's art.

Concept Books

Young children live in wonder. Their curiosity is all-consuming and all-encompassing. They want to know about everyone and everything. Informational books, usually in the form of concept books, can serve to satisfy many of these needs. Good concept books teach important, basic ideas or generalizations with scrupulous attention to accuracy. They adhere to one focus: material is presented simply, clearly, and without distraction. The text is brief and succinct; it is supported by appropriate illustration with attention given to freshness and originality of presentation. In doing all of this, concept books nurture more thought and wonder, and challenge children to generate yet more questions.

THE BABY'S CATALOGUE
Allan & Janet Ahlberg
Picture Puffins, 1984
Not so much a picture dictionary of everything that's important to baby, but rather, for baby and adult who share these pages, a book full of jokes, dialogues, anecdotes, and stories, to discover and to invent.
OTHER BOOKS: *Peek-A-Boo!*

BACK TO FRONT
Dick Bruna
Methuen, 1986
A first book of visual puzzles effectively rendered in Bruna's simple, stylized drawings.
OTHER BOOKS: *I Can Read; I Can Read More; I Can Read Difficult Words; I Can Make Music; I Know About Shapes; Find My Hat; My Shirt Is White; When I'm Big; My Sport Book; I Can Dress Myself; I Am a Clown; Dick Bruna's Word Book; Dick Bruna's Animal Book.*

BIKES
Anne Rockwell
Macmillan, 1987
A brief, poetic text and simple pictures tell all about this mode of transportation and recreation.
OTHER BOOKS: *Big Wheels; Boats; Cars; Fire Engines; Planes; Trucks; First Comes Spring; Can I Help?; Happy Birthday to Me; How My Garden Grew; I Love My Pets; I Play in My Room; Machines; My Barber; My Back Yard; Our Garage Sale; Sick in Bed; The Supermarket; The Toolbox; Thruway.*

BUILDING A HOUSE
Byron Barton
Picture Puffins, 1986
In simple illustrations that make use of broad, flat spaces, this picture book shows the steps that go into making a house.
OTHER BOOKS: *Airport; Trucks.*

CLUCK BAA
John Burningham
Walker, 1984
Daddies, puppies, buses, pigs. You will know them all by the sounds they make. Fun for baby and grownup to talk about as they pore over the pictures.
OTHER BOOKS: *Jangle Twang; Skip Trip; Slam Bang; Sniff Shout; Wobble Pop.*

COLOURS
Gillian Youldon
Watts, 1979
A first set of basic concept books, bright and effective.
OTHER BOOKS: *Numbers; Opposites; Sizes; Shapes; Time.*

FARM
Jan Pienkowski
Picture Puffins, 1986
Illustrations in vibrant colors outlined in black are the hallmark of this fine artist.
OTHER BOOKS: *ABC; Colours; Faces; Food; Homes; Numbers; Shapes; Sizes; Time; Zoo.*

FEELINGS
Aliki
Greenwillow Books, 1985
In miniature scenarios, illustrated with delicate line art, complemented by sharp comic-strip dialogue, Aliki explores the gamut of feelings young children experience in their everyday lives—anger, frustration, jealousy, pride, love, loneliness, and guilt.

FLYING
Donald Crews
Greenwillow Books, 1986
The poetry of his subject is what this picture book artist expresses in
this book about something ordinary that should give us cause to
wonder.
OTHER BOOKS: *Carousel; Freight Train; Harbor; Rain; School Bus; Truck;
Ten Black Dots.*

HELLO! GOODBYE!
Nigel McMullen
Macmillan, 1984
Funny, true to life stories built around baby's favorite words and
expressions.
OTHER BOOKS: *Never Mind!; Night, Night!; Oh Dear!*

I SEE
Rachel Isadora
Greenwillow Books, 1985
Pictures filled with joy and wonder illustrate a simple text about
familiar sights in a child's world.
SEQUELS: *I Hear; I Touch.*
OTHER BOOKS: *Backstage; Ben's Trumpet; My Ballet Class; Max; Opening
Night.*

IS IT RED? IS IT YELLOW? IS IT BLUE?
Tana Hoban
Greenwillow Books, 1978
Photography matched with simple, poetic text. The book teaches not
only color but also shape, size, texture, and relationships and,
perhaps most significantly, invites the reader to share in the beauty
of the everyday.
OTHER BOOKS: *Big Ones, Little Ones; Circles; Triangles and Squares;
Dig, Drill, Dump, Fill; Is It Larger? Is It Smaller?; Look Again!; Over,
Under and Through; Push, Pull, Empty, Full; A Book of Opposites; Shapes
and Things; Shapes, Shapes, Shapes; Take Another Look; What's That?;
Where Is It?*

MY DAY
Rod Campbell
William Collins Sons, 1986
The reader can look at the illustration and say the word—a
recognition book for babies.

MY VERY FIRST BOOK OF HOMES
Eric Carle
Thomas Y. Crowell, 1986
A fun mix-and-match book with split pages for matching up nest
with bird, hive with bee, cave with bat, and so on. Beautifully
illustrated, and sturdily made in light cardboard with plastic spiral
binding.
SERIES: *My Very First Book of Colours; My Very First Book of Food; My
Very First Book of Heads & Tails; My Very First Book of Letters; My Very
First Book of Motion; My Very First Book of Numbers; My Very First Book
of Shapes; My Very First Book of Sounds; My Very First Book of Tools; My
Very First Book of Touch.*

ON THE TOWN: A BOOK OF CLOTHING WORDS
Betsy and Giulio Maestro
Crown, 1975
The unlikely duo of elephant and master show preschoolers what the
well-dressed man, woman, and elephant wear over a night's and
day's activities on the town.
OTHER BOOKS: *Busy Day; On the Go; Harriet at Play; Harriet at School;
Harriet at Work.*

PEOPLE
Peter Spier
Doubleday, 1980
In oversize picture book format, with thousands of colored sketches,
Spier shows people everywhere on the globe, all of them different.
We are shown the many-faceted details of our differences in physical
appearance, clothing, homes, foods, religions, alphabets,
occupations, pastimes, etc.
OTHER BOOKS: *Crash! Bang! Boom!; Gobble, Growl, Grunt; Fast-Slow
High-Low.*

Alphabet Books

Alphabet books, like Mother Goose rhymes, were among the earliest books published for children, to teach the young their letters and provide them with moral instruction. Today these artistic creations, which are available in large numbers and a broad range and variety of subject and style, serve to provide children of all ages with much to look at, to think about and, when shared with an adult, to talk about. Alphabet books may be used to help children identify familiar objects, as well as letters and sounds; to understand and organize graphic experiences, and to develop their observational and discussion skills.

THE ABC BUNNY
Wanda Gag
Putnam Publishing Group, 1978
This classic is an example of an ABC built around a simple narrative: a bunny's alphabetical adventure begins as a falling apple wakes him up from his snug bed. Through the lilting verse and black and white woodcuts, the reader shares in a journey from A-Z.

A, B, SEE
Tana Hoban
Greenwillow Books, 1982
Through black and white photographs, Hoban introduces letters and reintroduces familiar objects. She encourages the reader to look, and look again.

B IS FOR BEAR: AN ABC
Dick Bruna
Methuen, 1972
A bright yellow bear, outlined in black, sits motionless against a red background. On the opposite page is a large black 'b'. Bruna's colorful artistry makes this a perfect book for the very young.

BY THE SEA: AN ALPHABET BOOK
Ann Blades
Kids Can Press, 1985
In this ABC created around a topical theme, small, primitive paintings in watercolors follow brother and sister through their seaside play and activities from morning to sunset. An example of an ABC that is a work of art with a strong sense of place—in this case, a West Coast beach.

JOHN BURNINGHAM'S ABC
John Burningham
Jonathan Cape, 1967
An example of the simplest kind of word-picture identification ABC.
On the left page are upper and lower case letters and one word: 'K
for King'. On the right page is a king reigning over his letter in
humorous Burningham style.

LIFT-THE-FLAP A B C
Rod Campbell
Blackie & Son, 1987
Young children will delight in lifting the flaps to discover the people,
animals, and things for every letter of the alphabet.

Counting Books

Counting books, like alphabet books, come in endless types, forms,
and styles. They range from those that present numbers in the
simplest manner, to those whose contents are related by theme or
tale, to those that serve as vehicles for aesthetic experiences of
various kinds rather than as concept books. Counting books are, of
course, no substitute for the young child's touching, playing with,
and manipulating real objects in order to learn basic mathematical
concepts—such as number sequence, one-to-one correspondence,
grouping, place value, and sets. But counting books are a vital
complement to these activities.

1, 2, 3,
Tana Hoban
Greenwillow Books, 1985
A first counting book which presents simple one to one
correspondence. The color photographs of objects familiar and
meaningful to the young child are labelled with the appropriate
numbers and names of the numerals.
OTHER BOOKS: *Count and See*

1 HUNTER
Pat Hutchins
Greenwillow Books, 1982
A counting book that is also a number story and a visual puzzle. A
hunter stalks hidden animals through the jungle. He misses them all,
although the observant reader can spot them behind their clever
camouflage, until the very last page when the animals come out of
hiding and the hunter runs away.

COUNT-UP
John Burningham
Viking Kestrel, 1983
The first of six flap books that introduce the pre-schooler to a variety of mathematical concepts and operations. In this book the child counts various animals; subsequent books in this series introduce the child to addition, subtraction, number combinations, numbers as signs, numbers as words, and so on.
SERIES: *Just Cats; Five Down; Pigs Plus; Read One; Ride Off.*

I CAN COUNT
Dick Bruna
Methuen, 1975
A simple counting book in the black-outlined classic illustrations of this beloved illustrator.
OTHER BOOKS: *I Can Count More; I Know More About Numbers.*

THE MOST AMAZING COUNTING BOOK
Robert Crowther
Viking Kestrel, 1979
Two spiders appear on the toadstool; four snails rise up from under the three rocks. On page after page of artful paper-engineering allied to inventive art-work and design, everything springs to life as the reader pulls tabs and lifts flaps.

NUMBERS OF THINGS
Helen Oxenbury
Heinemann, 1967
The first of this illustrator's great successes, this counting book remains a favorite for its colorful pages depicting numbers from one to fifty.

Themes: Hooray For Me

The books here celebrate the individuality that makes each of us unique, while at the same time affirming the idea of universality.

THE BAKED BEAN QUEEN
Rose Impey; ill. Sue Porter
Heinemann, 1986
A tale about a 'baddy' who eats baked beans for breakfast, and lunch, and supper. She never eats anything else; she's 'The Baked Bean Queen'. One of a series of witty stories about 'Baddies'. These are cautionary tales for parents rather than for children since, fortunately, the children always retain their integrity, and their dignity.
OTHER BOOKS: *The Bedtime Beast; The Demon Kevin; The Little Smasher; The Toothbrush Monster; Tough Teddy.*

BIG WORLD, SMALL WORLD
Jeanne Titherington
Greenwillow Books, 1985
A reminder that what is seen really depends on one's vantage point. Where Mama stops to talk to a neighbor, little Anna talks face-to-face with the neighbor's dog. The reader is given vignettes of a day with Anna and her mother, and is shown how the eyes of a child perceive the world in their own special way.

BREAD AND HONEY
Frank Asch
Parents Magazine Press, 1981
For Little Monkey's mother, a painting of her done at school by her own Little Monkey is perfect. Although every other animal offers Little Monkey advice, thinking there's just something missing from the painting, Mother Monkey epitomizes the truth that beauty is in the eye of the beholder.

HOORAY FOR ME!
Remy Charlip and Lilian Moore; ill. Vera Williams
Parent's Magazine Press, 1975
"Whatever we do, Whatever we be, Hooray for you, Hooray for me!" is the conclusion of this exploration and celebration of self, relationships, and who one is to oneself and to others.

HOW DO I PUT IT ON?
Shigeo Watanabe; ill. Yasuo Ohtomo
Philomel, 1977
Humor and charm are the qualities, in both text and illustrations, that make the daily life struggles of this young bear a perennial favorite with all small children. In this book, Bear manages to put his clothes on all the wrong parts of the body.
OTHER BOOKS: *Hallo, How Are You?; How Do I Eat It?; I Can Build a House!; I Can Do It!; I'm Playing with Papa!; I'm the King of the Castle; Ready, Steady, Go!*

MIFFY
Dick Bruna
Methuen, 1967
Miffy is Bruna's delightful character that takes the reader through the many experiences of early childhood. The illustrations are classically Bruna with simple shapes and outlines.
SEQUELS: *Miffy at School; Miffy at the Playground; Miffy at the Seaside; Miffy at the Zoo; Miffy Goes Flying; Miffy in Hospital; Miffy in the Snow; Miffy's Bicycle; Miffy's Birthday; Miffy's Dream.*
OTHER BOOKS: *Farmer John; Lisa and Lynn; Tilly and Tessa; The Apple; The Circus; The Egg; The Fish; The King; The Lifeboat; The Little Bird; The Sailor; The School.*

RED IS BEST
Kathy Stinson; ill. Robin Baird Lewis
Annick Press, 1982
The story of a toddler's obsessive love of the color red for all things, and of how she defends the color in the face of adult suggestions for alternative choices.
OTHER BOOKS: *Those Green Things; Big or Little.*

SWIMMY
Leo Lionni
Pantheon, 1963
A story about being different, about accepting those differences, and

about using them to face the perils of life, by one of the great fabulists of our day.
OTHER BOOKS: *A Color of His Own; Alexander and the Wind-Up Mouse; Frederick the Biggest Mouse in the World; Fish is Fish; Little Blue and Little Yellow; Pezzetino.*

TELL ME, GRANDMA, TELL ME, GRANDPA
Shirlee P. Newman; ill. Joan Drescher
Houghton Mifflin, 1979
A young girl curls up with her grandparents to hear about the time her mom and dad were children, and turns her imagination loose.

WHEN YOU WERE LITTLE AND I WAS BIG
Priscilla Galloway; ill. Heather Collins
Annick Press, 1984
A young child tells her mother a story about growing up from her own point of view.
OTHER BOOKS: *Good Times Bad Times Mummy and Me; Jennifer Has Two Daddies.*

WILLIAM'S DOLL
Charlotte Zolotow; ill. William Pene du Bois
Harper & Row Publishers, 1972
No one understands William's burning desire to have a doll of his own. No one, that is, except Grandma. Everyone else wants William to learn basketball, or to play with his toy train; but Grandma knows that a doll to hug will help William learn to be a good Dad one day. A wise book that makes a strong statement about individual differences.
OTHER BOOKS: *Someday*

Themes: The Daily Round

In these books, the focus is on the daily round of life, the small domestic dramas for the young child, the common experiences and events.

ASK MR. BEAR
Marjorie Flack
Macmillan, 1932
The little boy wants to give his mother a birthday present, and asks the animals for suggestions.

THE BLANKET
John Burningham
Jonathan Cape, 1974
The toddler can't find his blanket one night. How everyone joins in the search and who finds the blanket makes a reassuring story.
OTHER BOOKS: *The Baby; The Cupboard; The Dog; The Friend; The Rabbit; The School; The Snow.*

DOING THE WASHING
Sarah Garland
Bodley Head, 1983
The familiar household chore of washing clothes turned into an adventure for the young child.
SEQUELS: *Going Shopping; Having a Picnic; Coming to Tea.*

EARLY MORNING IN THE BARN
Nancy Tafuri
Greenwillow Books, 1983
A poem in praise of the early morning sights and sounds found in the barn.

EATING OUT
Helen Oxenbury
Walker, 1983
Sharp observation of people's foibles, especially in the face of life's minor trials and tribulations, coupled with an unerring ability to portray the daily round in a humorous way.
OTHER BOOKS: *Gran & Grampa; Our Dog; Playschool; The Birthday Party; The Check-Up; The Dancing Class; The Drive; The Visitor.*

AN EVENING AT ALFIE'S
Shirley Hughes
Bodley Head, 1984
Everything goes wrong the night Alfie and little sister are babysat. A funny nightmare in Hughes's spare prose and old-fashioned pictures.
SEQUELS: *Alfie Gives a Hand; Alfie Gets in First; Alfie's Feet.*

JAMIE'S STORY
Wendy Watson
Philomel, 1981
A toddler describes a day in his life as he helps his mother and father, plays, and discovers an exciting world around him. A funny text that uses only the words first learned by young children, complemented by watercolors.

NATURAL HISTORY
M.B. Goffstein
Farrar, Straus & Giroux, 1979
A small book with a powerful statement about the world we live in:
"Every living creature is our brother and our sister."

NOW WE CAN GO
Ann Jonas
Greenwillow Books, 1987
"Wait a minute! I'm not ready!" Anyone who has ever tried to leave
the house with a young child knows it cannot be done until certain
rituals are observed.
OTHER BOOKS: *Where Can It Be?*

WAKE UP, JEREMIAH
Ronald Himler
Harper & Row Publishers, 1979
In a flow of textured paintings and brief text this picture book
captures a child's greeting to the sun and a new day.

Themes: Friendship

Friendship is celebrated in this sampling of books—the importance of
friendship, its pervasiveness, its special qualities, its struggles, and
the measure of its worth.

A BAG FULL OF PUPS
Dick Gackenbach
Clarion Books, 1981
Everybody wants a puppy from the man who has a bag of pups to
give, but they all have an ulterior motive in wanting one—to train it
to do tricks for the circus, to teach it to be a watchdog, and so on.
Only the little boy wants a pup just to have as a friend and to love.

CORDUROY
Don Freeman
Viking, 1968
The story of a department store teddy bear's quest for a friend. An affirmation that one need not be perfect to be loved.
SEQUEL: *A Pocket for Corduroy*

GOING FOR A WALK (Original Title: THE LITTLE BOOK)
Beatrice Schenk de Regniers
Harper & Row Publishers, 1961
When a little girl goes for a walk, she meets a cow that says *Moo*, a rooster that says *Cock-a-doodle-doo*, and a pig that says *Oink*. But she finds out that the *Hi* of a new found playmate is the best sound of all.
OTHER BOOKS: *May I Bring a Friend?*

MAUDE AND SALLY
Nicki Weiss
Greenwillow Books, 1983
Two best friends are separated because one goes off to summer camp. When Sally goes away, Maude plays with Emmylou all summer; when Sally comes home, there is a change—but it's a change that makes everything even better.

A SPECIAL TRADE
Sally Whitman; ill. Karen Gundersheimer
Harper & Row Publishers, 1978
When the little girl is a baby, the elderly neighbor next door pushes her in her stroller every day; as she grows up and her old friend gets infirm, it is the little girl's turn to push the man in his wheelchair.

TIMOTHY GOES TO SCHOOL
Rosemary Wells
Dial Books, 1981
After a series of minor disasters, it's finding a friend that finally saves—and makes—Timothy's day.
OTHER BOOKS: *Benjamin and Tulip*

Themes: Family

These are books that look at the family—Mom, Dad, siblings, the new baby, grandparents, and all the relatives. These books celebrate the nurturing relationships in which we learn and grow. The complexity of family relationships is fully reflected: the satisfactions, the hurts, the joys, the sorrows—not omitting family breakup. The warm simplicity of family acceptance and companionship brings to the child in each of us a fuller understanding of those memorable relationships we each call 'family.'

DAD'S BACK
Jan Ormerod
Walker, 1986
This book and the others in the series are about babies and their fathers. Glimpses of family life are gentle, humorous, and true to life.
OTHER BOOKS: *Messy Baby; Reading; Sleeping.*

HAPPY FAMILIES
Allan and Janet Ahlberg and others
Picture Puffins, 1986
A brightly illustrated series of family stories, each focusing on an individual in a happy family.
SERIES: *Master Money the Millionaire; Master Salt the Sailor's Son; Miss Brick the Builder's Baby; Miss Jump the Jockey; Mr and Miss Hay the Horses; Mr Biff the Boxer; Mr Buzz the Beeman; Mr Cosmo the Conjuror; Mr Tick the Teacher; Mrs. Lather's Laundry; Mrs. Plug the Plumber; Mrs. Wobble the Waitress.*

I THINK HE LIKES ME
Elizabeth Winthrop; ill. Denise Saldutti
Harper & Row Publishers, 1980
The little girl is sure her new baby brother likes her although, it seems, whenever she wants to play with him, her parents tell her not to squeeze him too tight or not to wake him. But the day comes when the little girl proves herself with the baby who does indeed like her very much.

IF IT WEREN'T FOR YOU
Charlotte Zolotow; ill. Ben Shecter
Harper & Row Publishers, 1966
Spare text with pictures work together to make a tender poem to a sibling. A reaffirming book about brothers and sisters.

OTHER BOOKS: *Big Sister, Little Sister; Do You Know What I'll Do?; The Quarrelling Book; The Unfriendly Book; My Grandson Lew.*

ON MOTHER'S LAP
Ann Herbert Scott; ill. Glo Coalson
McGraw-Hill, 1972
A child learns that Mother's lap is a very special sort of place because it can make room for everyone.

THE VISITORS WHO CAME TO STAY
Annalena McAffee; ill. Anthony Browne
Hamilton, 1984
Katy lives alone with her Dad, and she likes it that way. When Dad brings home his new friend, Mary, and her son, Sean, life changes dramatically for Katy. Browne's surrealistic illustrations highlight a book which reminds us that while families may all be different, loving and giving is what a happy family is all about.

Themes: Reassuring Books

Children of all ages, but particularly young children, need and enjoy stories that provide reassurance and give comfort. These are the books that, ultimately, foster a positive self-image. In promoting self-regard, these are the books that enable children to love themselves and thus love others.

THE LAST PUPPY
Frank Asch
Prentice-Hall, 1980
He was the last of nine puppies; the last one to open his eyes, the last to learn to drink from a saucer, the last one into the doghouse at night. With simplicity and warmth, this book shows that being last, being left out, being in someone else's shadow is not the end—often it means something very special.
OTHER BOOKS: *Just Like Daddy*

LITTLE GORILLA
Ruth Bornstein
Seabury, 1976
Everybody loved Little Gorilla. Then Little Gorilla began to grow, and grow, and grow, until one day Little Gorilla was big. A story about the security and constancy of love.

THE RUNAWAY BUNNY
Margaret Wise Brown; ill. Clement Hurd
Harper & Row Publishers, 1942
Little bunny plays a game of hide-and-seek with his mother. As often as he runs away, his mother finds him and is there for him with a hug.
OTHER BOOKS: *Little Chicken*

SOME THINGS GO TOGETHER
Charlotte Zolotow; ill. Karen Gundersheimer
Thomas Y. Crowell, 1983
As every young child knows, some things naturally go together—franks with beans, kings with queens. But best of all, there's you with me. Playful verses decorated with detailed pictures that work well together.
OTHER BOOKS: *Say It!*

Themes: Solving Problems

Perhaps every good story has at its heart a difficulty to be surmounted, a problem to be solved. The books listed here deal with these a little more overtly, and show how children cope with life's vicissitudes. These books also touch on the physical, intellectual, and emotional changes children must adjust to as they grow up.

BUT NOT BILLY
Charlotte Zolotow; ill. Kay Chorao
Harper & Row Publishers, 1983
A mother nicknamed her baby, Billy, all kinds of pet names—little duck, little pigeon, little bunny, or whatever creature he looked or sounded like—until the day he said "Mama." On that day the infant becomes "Billy." A book about growing into a name and an identity.
OTHER BOOKS: *Someone New; The Sky was Blue.*

THE CARROT SEED
Ruth Krauss; ill. Crockett Johnson
Harper & Row Publishers, 1945
A boy plants a carrot and believes it will grow despite the disbelief
of his family. A book about the importance of persistence, an
enduring theme in children's books, and of faith.

HAPPY BIRTHDAY, SAM
Pat Hutchins
Bodley Head, 1978
On his birthday, Sam finds that although he's a whole year older
he's no bigger. He still can't reach the light switch, or the clothes in
his closet, or the door knob when there's a knock at the front door.
But Grandpa's present that the postman brings to the door solves all
Sam's problems.
OTHER BOOKS: *Titch; You'll Soon Grow Into Them, Titch.*

HOLES AND PEEKS
Ann Jonas
Greenwillow Books, 1984
Holes can be scary when you're little. But peeks, openings you can
make yourself, are fun. And holes can be plugged or patched or
made smaller so they're no longer scary. A reassuring book about
some of the child's fears about everyday, ordinary things.
OTHER BOOKS: *The Trek*

I WAS SO MAD
Karen Erickson; ill. Maureen Roffey
Penguin, 1986
A lively and amusing story. The stories in this series show children
taking their first steps in understanding their emotions and feelings
and overcoming some practical difficulty or problem.
SERIES: *I Can Do Something When There's Nothing To Do; I Can Get
Organized; I Can Settle Down; I Can Share; I'll Try; It's Dark—But I'm
Not Scared; No One is Perfect.*

JULIE STAYS THE NIGHT
Nigel Snell
Hamish Hamilton, 1982
Written in an amusing but empathic style, this story and the others
in this useful series looks at the facts behind common events or
experiences that may cause a young child anxiety or distress.
SERIES: *Ann Visits the Speech Therapist; Clare's New Baby Brother; Danny*

is Afraid of the Dark; David's First Day at School; Emma's Cat Dies; George Gets Chicken-pox; Jane has Asthma; Jason Breaks his Arm; Jenny Learns to Swim; Johnny Gets Some Glasses; Kate Visits the Doctor; Lucy Loses her Tonsils; Mark Gets Nits; Martin Feels Lonely; Paul Gets Lost; Peter Gets a Hearing Aid; Ruth Goes to Hospital; Sally Moves House; Sam's New Dad; Steve is Adopted; Sue Learns to Cross the Road; Tom Visits the Dentist.

LEO THE LATE BLOOMER
Robert Kraus; ill. Jose Arvego
Windmill Books, 1972
This classic fable about growing up demonstrates the slowness of the process.
OTHER BOOKS: Milton the Early Riser; Owliver; The Little Giant.

NOBODY LISTENS TO ANDREW
Elizabeth Guilfoile; ill. Mary Stevens
Follett, 1957
Andrew has something important to tell, but nobody will listen. A surprise ending.

NOISY NORA
Rosemary Wells
Dial Books, 1973
A middle child mouse likes to make a lot of noise to get her fair share of attention, but learns that she gets more notice when she is absolutely quiet.
OTHER BOOKS: A Lion for Lewis

PETEY
Tobi Tobias; ill. Symeon Shimin
Putnam's Publishing Group, 1978
Petey was a part of Emily's day. When she came home from school, the little gerbil was always there in his cage, waiting for her. And now Petey was dying. Charcoal illustrations complementing a credible story show that to accept death is to begin to understand that life changes and continues.

Themes: First Adventures

Young children love adventure. Here is a sampling of books that represent the very best of different kinds of adventure: setting out and arriving, seeking and finding, and traveling far to find what is near, to mention only a few.

CHICKEN FORGETS
Miska Miles
Little, Brown & Company, 1976
Mother Hen's shopping list is quite simple: a basket of berries. "Don't forget," she admonishes her chick. After various memory lapses and detours, the chick returns triumphant with the berries and pride in his accomplishment.

CLEVER BILL
William Nicholson
FSG, 1977
A simple story of the toy soldier who gets left behind when the little girl goes away to the seaside, and how his faithfulness saves the day.

DOGGER
Shirley Hughes
Bodley Head, 1977
The suspenseful story of the loss of a soft brown toy dog called Dogger and how his faithful master Dave tracks him down. The picture book that won this author-illustrator the Kate Greenaway Medal.

GOOD MORNING, CHICK
Mirra Ginsburg; ill. Byron Barton
Greenwillow Books, 1980
Chick comes out of his egg, learns to eat worms, seeds, and crumbs, and then his adventures begin.

MR. GUMPY'S OUTING
John Burningham
Jonathan Cape, 1970
Assorted animals get a dunking when they don't heed Mr. Gumpy's warnings about how to behave in a very full boat. A cumulative tale with scratchily painted pictures full of humor.
SEQUEL: *Mr. Gumpy's Motor Car*
OTHER BOOKS: *Borka: The Adventures of a Goose With No Feathers; Cannonball Simp; Humbert, Mr. Firkin & The Lord Mayor of London; Trubloff.*

Themes: Scary Books

As they grow and become independent, older toddlers and preschoolers enjoy scary stories, books that explore—and assuage— their many and various anxieties and fears, real or imagined.

ANGRY ARTHUR
Hiawyn Oram; ill. Satoshi Kitamura
Andersen, 1982
Not being allowed to watch his favorite TV program makes Arthur very angry. Arthur gets so angry that some astonishing things begin to happen.

GILA MONSTERS MEET YOU AT THE AIRPORT
Marjorie Sharmat; ill. Byron Barton
Macmillan, 1980
What happens when the little boy is afraid of moving and (naturally) expects the very worst—including gila monsters.

I'M COMING TO GET YOU
Tony Ross
Andersen, 1984
"I'm coming to get you!" hisses the terrible monster from outer space, as it speeds on its way towards a planet called Earth. It's going to get little Tommy Brown, who happens to be particularly scared of monsters. But there's a twist in this story, which turns it into a powerful parable about the fears and problems in our lives.
OTHER BOOKS: *Lazy Jack*

MY MAMA SAYS THERE AREN'T ANY ZOMBIES, GHOSTS, VAMPIRES, CREATURES, DEMONS, MONSTERS, FIENDS, GOBLINS, OR THINGS
Judith Viorst; ill. Kay Chorao
Atheneum, 1973
Even though the little boy's Mother assures him that his fear of monsters is quite unfounded he is not comforted. Children love to chant the refrain throughout: "Sometimes even mamas make mistakes."

WHERE THE WILD THINGS ARE
Maurice Sendak
Harper & Row Publishers, 1963
For many, both adults and children, this classic is their favorite picture book. Naughty Max, sent to bed without his supper, runs away to have a good time in the land of the wild things. In the end, he comes back home where they love him best of all, and his hot supper is waiting for him.

Themes: Animal Books

Children enjoy stories in which animals act like people—often like small children. In these stories the animals look like, live like, and behave like children and, most important, face their situations and problems.

CURIOUS GEORGE
H.A. Rey
Houghton Mifflin, 1941
George, the little monkey whose curiosity always gets him into trouble, and his owner, the kind man with the yellow hat, have been delighting children for nearly fifty years. A classic series.
SERIES: *Curious George and the Dump Truck; Curious George Flies a Kite; Curious George Gets a Medal; Curious George Goes to the Aquarium; Curious George Goes to the Circus; Curious George Goes Sledding; Curious George Goes to the Hospital; Curious George Learns the Alphabet; Curious George Rides a Bike; Curious George Takes a Job.*

FIRST FLIGHT
David McPhail
Little, Brown & Company, 1987
A naughty teddy bear ignores all the rules of safety and behavior while traveling on his first airplane flight.
SEQUELS: *A Kiss for Little Bear; Little Bear; Little Bear's Friend; Little Bear's Visit.*

GREGORY'S DOG
William Stobbs
Oxford University Press, 1984
Gregory says, "Sit," Gregory says, "Fetch," but Gregory's dog always does the opposite of what his young master says, except when Gregory says "Eat." In thin colors over rough canvas texture.
SEQUEL: *Gregory's Garden*

HARRIET'S HALLOWEEN CANDY
Nancy Carlson
Carolrhoda, 1982
Quite determined not to share her Halloween treats with her little brother, Walt, Harriet soon runs out of places to hide them. This author-illustrator has created delightful and distinctive characters in Harriet and Walt, Loudmouth George, Louanne Pig, and others.
SERIES: *Harriet & the Garden; Harriet & the Roller Coaster; Harriet's Recital; Harriet & Walt; Loudmouth George & the Big Race; Loudmouth George & the New Neighbours; Loudmouth George & the Sixth-Grade Bully; Louanne Pig in Making the Team; Louanne Pig in the Mysterious Valentine; Louanne Pig in the Perfect Family; Louanne Pig in the Talent Show; Louanne Pig in the Witch Lady.*

HARRY THE DIRTY DOG
Gene Zion; ill. Margaret B. Graham
Harper & Row Publishers, 1956
Children readily identify with the weaknesses of this famous little white dog with black spots. Simple story-line and illustrations make this book and its sequels suitable for the youngest.
SEQUELS: *Harry and the Lady Next Door; Harry By the Sea; No Roses for Harry.*

THE HOUSE ON EAST 88TH STREET
Bernard Waber
Houghton Mifflin, 1962
From the bathtub of the Primm family's new apartment come the sounds, swish, swash, splash, swoosh. And then they see it—a

gigantic crocodile. Lyle, the crocodile, comes into their lives never to leave them the same again.
SEQUELS: *Lyle and the Birthday Party; Lyle Finds His Mother; Lyle, Lyle Crocodile.*
OTHER BOOKS: *An Anteater Named Arthur*

KATE'S BOX
Kay Chorao
E.P. Dutton Books, 1982
Little adventures about Kate the elephant, told in fifty words or less with humor and understanding.
SEQUELS: *Kate's Car; Kate's Quilt; Kate's Snowman.*

MRS. PIG GETS CROSS & OTHER STORIES
Mary Rayner
William Collins Sons, 1986
More stories about Mother and Father Pig and their irrepressible piggy children—Sorrell, Bryony, Hilary, Sarahy, Toby, Cindy, William, Alun, Bejamin, and Garth.
SEQUELS: *Garth Pig & the Ice Cream Lady; Mr. & Mrs. Pig's Evening Out; Mrs. Pig's Bulk Buy.*

THE STORY ABOUT PING
Marjorie Flack; ill. Kurt Wiese
Viking, 1933
Ping, the duckling, does not want to take his spanking for being last on his family's boat, so he hides from his family by staying out all night. He nearly gets caught for someone's supper. The grief he thus endures makes the requisite spanking a small sacrifice for being reunited with his family.
OTHER BOOKS: *Angus and the Cat; Angus Lost; Angus and the Ducks.*

THROUGH THE YEAR WITH BORIS BEAR
Dick Bruna
Methuen, 1987
A new character from this classic author-illustrator. These small-format books with simple text are accompanied by bold line drawings of solid colors. All about the life of Boris Bear, with whom children will readily identify.
OTHER BOOKS: *Poppy Pig; Poppy Pig Goes to Market; Poppy Pig's Birthday; Poppy Pig's Garden; Pussy Nell; Snuffy; Snuffy and the Fire; Snuffy's Dream.*

Themes: Bedtime Books

Books for bedtime don't have to be about going to sleep—any kind of book may be part of a toddler's goodnight ritual. Nevertheless, there is a special quality about some bedtime books that provide a child with the warmth, comfort, and reassurance to face the dark alone.

A CHILD'S BOOK OF PRAYERS
Michael Hague
Holt, Rinehart & Winston, 1985
An illustrated collection containing more than twenty of the best-loved prayers, from the Lord's Prayer to "Now I lay me down to sleep."

GOODNIGHT, GOODNIGHT
Eve Rice
Greenwillow Books, 1980
A soothing text set against a striking black and white cityscape, touched with bright yellow from the light of the moon, tells how goodnight creeps through the city, finally coming to the kitten whose mother takes it home.

GOODNIGHT MOON
Margaret Wise Brown; ill. Clement Hurd
Harper & Row Publishers, 1947
A little rabbit bids goodnight to all the things in her room; gradually the room darkens until only the light of the moon may be seen when, at last, she falls asleep. A gentle, soothing tone poem accompanied by haunting illustrations.
OTHER BOOKS: *The Goodnight Moon Room; A Child's Goodnight Book.*

HERE A LITTLE CHILD I STAND
Satomi Ichikawa
Heinemann, 1982
Children from all cultures, Islamic to Hebrew, Inuit to Japanese, offer simple, beautiful prayers.

PRAYER FOR A CHILD
Rachel Field; ill. Elizabeth Orton Jones
Macmillan, 1945
A gentle prayer with nostalgic illustrations. Winner of the Caldecott Medal.

SEE THE MOON
Robert Kraus
Windmill, 1980
A bedtime boardbook with a yellow moon and stars that glow in the dark.

TEN, NINE, EIGHT
Molly Bang
Greenwillow Books, 1983
Bold colors and strong rhythms combine in this affectionate bedtime book about a black father and child counting backwards from ten little toes to one big girl all ready for bed.

Read-Aloud Picture Story Books and First Novels

Preschool children, as they mature, need a variety of read-aloud and shared-book experiences to enrich their literary understandings and to extend their listening skills. Here is a sampling, ranging from picture books that are more complex and difficult, to picture story books—in which pictures are secondary to text—to collections of linked short stories, first 'chapter books' or novels, and novel series.

FANTASTIC MR. FOX
Roald Dahl; ill. Jill Bennett
Allen & Unwin, 1967
Boggis, Bunce, and Bean are three "wicked and cruel and mean" farmers who are determined to kill Mr. Fox. However, in this fast-paced story, Mr. Fox is far too clever for them because, as Mrs. Fox proudly reminds her young ones: ". . .I'd like you to know that your father is a *fantastic* fox!"
OTHER BOOKS: *The Magic Finger; The Enormous Crocodile.*

THE LITTLES
John Peterson
Scholastic, 1970
A series of first novels for young readers. Within these short

chapters is fast-paced reading exploring the fascination of "little people." The Littles are a colony of six-inch people who live inside the walls of the Bigg family's house. Their daily lives are full of adventures warding off giant mice, cats, etc. while still keeping their existence a secret from the Bigg family.

SERIES: *The Littles and the Big Storm; The Littles and Their Friends; The Littles and the Trash Tinnies; The Littles Go to School; The Littles Have a Wedding; The Littles' Surprise Party; The Littles to the Rescue; Tom Little's Great Halloween Scare.*

MY NAUGHTY LITTLE SISTER AND BAD HARRY
Dorothy Edwards; ill. Shirley Hughes
A collection of stories about Naughty Little Sister and her friend, Bad Harry. These two get into all kinds of mischief, from trouble on Mother's washing day to adventures at the library.

SERIES: *My Naughty Little Sister; My Naughty Little Sister's Friends; When My Naughty Little Sister was Good; My Naughty Little Sister Goes Fishing; My Naughty Little Sister and Bad Harry's Rabbit; My Naughty Little Sister at the Fair.*

THE ORIGINAL PETER RABBIT BOOKS
Beatrix Potter
Warne, 1902-1922
The first story in this series, *The Tale of Peter Rabbit*, is a classic tale about a disobedient rabbit. Potter's small format, detailed drawings, and suspenseful prose combine to create a miniature world that reflects the realities, needs, and feelings of all children.

SERIES: *The Tale of Peter Rabbit; The Tale of Squirrel Nutkin; The Tailor of Gloucester; The Tale of Benjamin Bunny; The Tale of Two Bad Mice; The Tale of Mrs. Tiggy-Winkle; The Tale of Mr. Jeremy Fisher; The Tale of Tom Kitten; The Tale of Jemima Puddle-Duck; The Tale of the Flopsy Bunnies; The Tale of Mrs. Tittlemouse; The Tale of Timmy Tiptoes; The Tale of Johnny Town-Mouse; The Tale of Mr. Tod; The Tale of Pigling Bland; The Tale of Samuel Whiskers; The Pie and Patty-Pan; Ginger and Pickles; The Tale of Little Pig Robinson; The Story of a Fierce Bad Rabbit; The Story of Miss Moppet.*

THE STORY OF BABAR, THE LITTLE ELEPHANT
Jean de Brunhoff
Random House, 1960
The classic tales of the kindly King Babar and his wife Celeste, their lovable children and relatives, and all their adventures and misadventures. The Babar series was extended by Jean de Brunhoff's son, Laurent, who published his first title *Babar's Cousin*, on his

father's death, and has since published over two dozen more titles, mostly short stories in small format.
SEQUELS: *The Travels of Babar; Babar the King; Babar's ABC; Babar's Friend Zephir; Babar at Home; Babar and Father Christmas.*

TIM ALL ALONE
Edward Ardizzone
Oxford University Press, 1956
Little Tim goes on seafaring adventures in which he and his companions face perils and overcome great odds before returning to the warmth and security of home. This title was the winner of the first Kate Greenaway Medal awarded for its pen and ink illustrations splashed with watercolors.
SEQUELS: *Little Tim & The Brave Sea Captain; Ship's Cook Ginger; Tim & Charlotte; Tim & Ginger; Tim & Lucy Go to Sea; Tim in Danger; Tim's Friend Towser; Tim's Last Voyage; Tim to the Lighthouse; Tim to the Rescue.*

WARTON AND MORTON
Russell Erickson; ill. Lawrence Di Fiori
Dell Publishing Co., 1977
Morton and Warton are two domesticated brother toads who approach life and adventure in very different ways. In all these stories, there is humor, adventure, and courage, as well as the bonds of brotherhood.
SERIES: *A Toad for Tuesday; Warton and the Castaways; Warton and the King of the Skies; Warton and the Traders; Warton's Christmas Eve Adventure.*

Traditional Tales

Folk and fairy tales, writes American critic Betsy Hearne, ''are the bare bones of story. Each archetypal character represents a part of humanity, each action a part of life, each setting a part of existence.'' Here is a sampling of this ageless literature that is the rightful heritage of every child.

ARDIZZONE'S HANS ANDERSEN
Stephen Corrin; ill. Edward Ardizzone
Atheneum, 1971
This collection of fourteen tales includes favorites from the work of Hans Christian Andersen. Ardizzone's subtle color wash and delicate

black and white drawings capture the essence of Andersen's storytelling.

CINDERELLA
Dick Bruna
Methuen, 1967
A fairy tale for the very youngest, recreated in simple words and pictures that manage to retain the story's heart and integrity.
OTHER BOOKS: *Hop-O'-My Thumb; Red Riding Hood; Snow White; The Christmas Book.*

THE FAIRY TALE TREASURY
Virginia Haviland; ill. Raymond Briggs
Coward, 1972
A now classic collection of thirty-two well loved fairy tales, from Henny Penny to Mollie Whuppie. All are illustrated with robust humor.

GOLDILOCKS AND THE THREE BEARS
Lorinda Bryan Cauley
Putnam Publishing Group, 1980
A retelling of this classic tale about a mischievous little girl and three surprised bears. Cauley's characters are humorously portrayed and her detailed paintings complement the text.
OTHER BOOKS: *The Three Little Pigs; The Cock, The Mouse and the Little Red Hen; The Ugly Duckling; Jack and the Bean Stalk.*

HANSEL AND GRETEL
Jacob Grimm; ill. Susan Jeffers
Dial Books, 1980
Jeffers' larger-than-life illustrations enhance this suspenseful tale about two abandoned children who discover a house that is wonderful beyond their dreams.
OTHER BOOKS: *Thumbelina; Snow White and the Seven Dwarfs; The Wild Swans; Hiawatha.*

THE HELEN OXENBURY NURSERY STORY BOOK
Helen Oxenbury
Heinemann, 1985
A sizable collection of the classic traditional tales, simply told and drolly illustrated.
OTHER BOOKS: *The Great Big Enormous Turnip*

LITTLE RED RIDING HOOD
Jacob Grimm; ill. Trina Schart Hyman
Holiday, 1983
A little girl ventures out to grandmother's house and meets up with a sly, hungry wolf. Hyman's draughtsmanship and skilled use of light and shadow illuminate rustic interiors and lush woodlands, capturing the drama as it unfolds.
OTHER BOOKS: *The Sleeping Beauty; Snow White.*

SNOW WHITE AND THE SEVEN DWARFS
Jacob Grimm; trans. Randall Jarell; ill. Nancy Ekholm Burket
FSG, 1972
The story of Snow White and the struggle between good and evil are re-enacted through Burkert's mediaeval illustrations.

THE THREE BEARS & 15 OTHER STORIES
Anne Rockwell
Thomas Y. Crowell, 1975
A first collection of traditional tales in prose matched by lambent illustrations.
OTHER BOOKS: *The Old Woman and Her Pig & 10 Other Stories*

THE THREE BILLY GOATS GRUFF
William Stobbs
Bodley Head, 1974
The three billy goats use their wits to defeat the evil troll who lives under the bridge. Stobbs' scratchy oil paintings accompany his retellings for the very youngest.
OTHER BOOKS: *The Story of the Three Bears; The Story of the Three Little Pigs; The Crock of Gold; The Hare and the Frogs; Henny Penny; The House that Jack Built.*

THE THREE LITTLE PIGS
Paul Galdone
Seabury, 1970
"I'll huff and I'll puff and I'll blow your house in," roars the wicked wolf. And that's what he does . . . until one clever and industrious pig outwits him.
OTHER BOOKS: *Henny Penny; Little Red Riding Hood; Little Tupen; Old Mother Hubbard and Her Dog; The Gingerbread Boy; The History of Simple Simon; The House that Jack Built; The Little Red Hen; The Magic Porridge Pot; The Old Woman and Her Pig; The Princess and the Pea; The Three Bears; The Three Billy Goats Gruff; The Teeny Tiny Woman; Tom, Tom, the Piper's Son.*

The Primary Years

How children feel about books alters in the primary years because they begin the process of learning to read. The fact that their ability to understand and their need for complex, meaningful stories don't match their reading skills may lead to frustration or eventually the abandoning of books altogether. Since the task of learning to read can be a difficult one for many children, it is important that adults continue to read aloud to them from as rich a selection of books as possible. Children must be encouraged to see in books a world of excitement and satisfaction. As they listen to powerful stories, look at and listen to wonderful picture books, join in with songs and poems, and discover information within non-fiction, they will be building the necessary vocabulary, story systems, and experiences that will serve them well as they become independent readers. The initial enthusiasm that beginning readers feel about reading must be supported by high quality easy readers and balanced by stories and books rich in language and image. Adults who understand the reading process will continue to share good books with children, extending their young worlds, modelling a love of books, developing language strengths, and building an atmosphere of trust and appreciation.

A wide variety of books are listed in this section because the primary years cover a wide range of both interests and abilities. Suggestions are given for books that adults can share with children—picture books, poems, collections, and information books—and materials that children can begin to read on their own—easy-to-read books, series books, school anthologies, chapter books, and first novels. There are books that are popular with many children, classics that have lasted over the years, and new examples of high-quality literature. Adults must be careful to match children with books that they want to read and that they can also handle—a difficult task but a vital one. These lists will be of benefit as the children develop from five and six-year-old beginning readers into strong, independent eight and nine-year-old readers.

Picture Books for Sharing

A child's reading strength is dependent on his or her experiences, both in life and in print. By sharing a picture book with a child on the lap or with a group, an adult can bring the words alive. At the same time the child can make sense of the pictures or illustrations as word and image blend to make meaning. The sharing of child and adult as they experience a book also builds a special bond that will strengthen the reading process. There are picture books of every type that will meet the needs of particular children. While picture books generally are not read by the child, they provide the print experiences that will lead to independent reading.

BEST FRIENDS
Steven Kellogg
Dial Books, 1986
Kathy feels lonely and betrayed when her best friend goes away for the summer without her.
OTHER BOOKS: *Pinkerton, Behave!; Tallyho Pinkerton!; A Rose for Pinkerton; Prehistoric Pinkerton; Chicken Little; Pecos Bill; Ralph's Secret Weapon; The Mysterious Tadpole; Can I Keep Him?; Much Bigger Than Martin; Won't Somebody Play with Me?; The Boy Who Was Followed Home; The Island of the Skog; The Mystery of the Stolen Blue Paint; The Mystery of the Missing Red Mitten.*

BIG SARAH'S LITTLE BOOTS
Paulette Bourgeois; ill. Brenda Clark
Kids Can Press, 1987
Sarah loves her yellow boots but she discovers one day that they just won't fit anymore. She must choose new ones and pass on her others to her younger brother.
OTHER BOOKS: *Franklin In the Dark*

BRAVE IRENE
William Steig
Farrar, Straus & Giroux, 1986
Irene's mother isn't feeling well enough to deliver the beautiful ball gown she's made for the duchess to wear that very evening. So Irene volunteers to get the gown to the palace on time, in spite of the fierce snowstorm that's brewing.
OTHER BOOKS: *Gorky Rises; Caleb and Kate; Solomon and the Rusty Nail; Sylvester and the Magic Pebble; Amos and Boris; The Amazing Bone; Rotten Island; Doctor de Soto; Tiffky Doofky.*

CAT & CANARY
Michael Foreman
Dial Books, 1985
Cat wishes he could fly like his best friend Canary. When he is whisked away by a kite, his wish comes true.
OTHER BOOKS: *Dinosaurs and All That Rubbish; Moose; War and Peas; Panda's Puzzle; All the King's Horses.*

CHERRIES AND CHERRY PITS
Vera B. Williams
Greenwillow Books, 1986
The central character, Bidemmi, draws pictures from her life's experiences and invents stories around them.
OTHER BOOKS: *A Chair for My Mother; Something Special for Me; Music For Everyone.*

CHIN CHIANG AND THE DRAGON'S DANCE
Ian Wallace
Douglas & McIntyre, 1984
Chin Chiang worries about whether he can dance the important dragon's dance and win his grandfather's approval.
OTHER BOOKS: *The Sparrow's Song; Very Last First Time.*

CRICTOR
Tomi Ungerer
Harper Trophy, 1983
Crictor, the boa constrictor is a very helpful pet—especially when there are burglars around.
OTHER BOOKS: *Snail, Where Are You?; One, Two, Where's My Shoe?; The Beast of Monsieur Racine; Zeralda's Ogre; Moon Man; Allumette; The Three Robbers; I am Papa Snap and these are my Favourite No Such Stories.*

HAVE YOU SEEN JOSEPHINE?
Stéphane Poulin
Tundra Books, 1986
Josephine, the cat, always spends time with her owner Daniel, unless it is Saturday. One Saturday, however, Daniel decides to find out what Josephine is up to and follows her on the streets of Montreal.
OTHER BOOKS: *A Beautiful City ABC; Can You Catch Josephine.*

MILTON THE EARLY RISER
Robert Kraus; ill. Jose and Ariane Aruego
Windmill Books, 1972
Milton, a panda bear, wakes up too early and causes a great deal of trouble.
OTHER BOOKS: *Herman the Helper; Owliver; Whose Mouse Are You?; Leo the Late Bloomer.*

MISS NELSON IS MISSING
Harry Allard; ill. James Marshall
Scholastic, 1977
Miss Nelson's class always misbehaves. When she is absent her replacement, Miss Viola Swamp, makes the class work so hard they wish Miss Nelson would come back.
SEQUELS: *Miss Nelson Is Back; Miss Nelson Has a Field Day.*
OTHER BOOKS: *Bumps in the Night; It's So Nice to Have a Wolf Around the House; Yummers; The Tutti Fruitti Case; There's a Party at Mona's Tonight.*

MISS RUMPHIUS
Barbara Cooney
Penguin, 1982
Alice Rumphius wants to travel the world when she grows up and then live by the sea—just as her grandfather had done. He told her, however, that she must do something to make the world more beautiful, and young Alice does not yet know what to do. Winner of the American Book Award.
OTHER BOOKS: *Chanticleer and the Fox; The Ox-Cart Man.*

NEXT YEAR I'LL BE SPECIAL
Patricia Reilly Giff; ill. Marylin Hafner
E.P. Dutton Books, 1980
Marilyn describes how much different life will be next year when she is in the second grade.
OTHER BOOKS: *Today Was A Terrible Day; The Most Awful Play.*

NO NEED FOR MONTY
James Stevenson
Greenwillow Books, 1987
Convinced that crossing the river on the back of Monty the alligator is too slow, the animals try to find a quicker way for their children to go to school.
OTHER BOOKS: *Worse than Willy!; Could Be Worse; That Dreadful Day; What's Under My Bed?; The Worst Person in the World.*

OUR SNOWMAN
M.B. Goffstein
Harper & Row Publishers, 1986
The morning after the first big blizzard, when the snow is heavy and white, a small girl and her younger brother decide to build a snowman.
OTHER BOOKS: *Brookie and Her Lamb; My Noah's Ark; An Artist; A Writer.*

PET SHOW!
Ezra Jack Keats
Collier Books, 1972
Everyone is on the way to the neighborhood pet show except Archie's cat who has just disappeared, leaving Archie without an entry.
OTHER BOOKS: *Hi, Cat!; Goggles; Whistle for Willie; Apt. 3; The Snowy Day; Regards to the Man in the Moon; The Trip.*

PROFESSOR NOAH'S SPACESHIP
Brian Wildsmith
Oxford University Press, 1980
When a strange sadness overcame the forest, the animals decided to leave on Professor Noah's amazing spaceship in search of a better world.
OTHER BOOKS: *What the Moon Saw; The Lion and the Rat; The North Wind and the Sun; The Rich Man and the Shoemaker; The Hare and The Tortoise; The Miller, the Boy and the Donkey; The Little Wood Duck; Python's Party; Mother Goose; Daisy; Goat's Trail; The Cat Sat on the Mat; Brian Wildsmith's ABC.*

STREGA NONA
Tomie de Paola
Prentice-Hall, 1975
All the townspeople come to Strega Nona for potions, cures, magic, and comfort. When she hires Big Anthony to look after her house and garden, the boy thinks he has discovered her magic secrets. A Caldecott Honor Book.
SEQUELS: *Big Anthony and the Magic Ring; Strega Nona's Magic Lessons; Merry Christmas, Strega Nona.*
OTHER BOOKS: *Pancakes for Breakfast; Helga's Dowry: A Troll Love Story; Nona Upstairs, Nona Downstairs; Now One Foot, Now the Other; Watch Out for the Chicken Feet in Your Soup; The Popcorn Book; The Cloud Book; The Legend of the Bluebonnet.*

THERE'S AN ALLIGATOR UNDER MY BED
Mercer Mayer
Dial Books, 1987
The alligator under his bed makes a boy's bedtime difficult until he lures it out of the house and into the garage.
SEQUELS: *There's a Nightmare in my Closet; What Do You Do With a Kangeroo?*

TWO DONKEYS AND A BRIDGE
Ralph Steadman
Andersen Press, 1983
Every day Dimitri and Theo, each with their donkeys, meet by the river. Their fathers, neighboring mayors, agree to build a bridge so the two boys and the two villages can become friends.
OTHER BOOKS: *Emergency Mouse; Inspector Mouse.*

WHERE'S JULIUS?
John Burningham
Jonathan Cape, 1986
Julius's parents never know where he is. He's busy digging a hole to the other side of the world or perhaps bathing hippos in the Lombo Bombo River.
OTHER BOOKS: *Borka; ABC; Seasons; Mr. Gumpy's Outing; Mr. Gumpy's Motor Car; Around the World in Eighty Days; Come Away from the Water, Shirley; Time to Get Out of the Bath, Shirley; Would You Rather...; The Shopping Basket; Avocado Baby; Granpa; Cannonball Simp.*

Wordless Books

By definition, a wordless book holds no difficulties for non-readers or beginning readers. Through the visuals, children have the opportunity to provide their own story line, dialogue, and characterization. These books will give the young reader strength in thought and imagination, and encourage participation within the book experience.

THE ANGEL AND THE SOLDIER BOY
Peter Collington
Alfred A. Knopf, 1987
A child dreams that her toy angel and soldier have the adventure of retrieving a stolen coin from pirates.

THE EXPEDITION
Willi Baum
Barron's Educational Series, 1975
This witty book depicts the problems of colonizing the people of a remote island when a ship of explorers arrives.

THE GIFT
John Prater
Bodley Head, 1985
Two young children receive a mysterious parcel and become more interested in the box than its contents.

THE SNOWMAN
Raymond Briggs
Random House, 1978
A wordless picture book which describes the dream-like adventures of a boy who thinks his snowman has come to life.
OTHER BOOKS: *Father Christmas; Father Christmas Goes on Holiday.*

WHERE'S WALDO?
Martin Handford
Little, Brown & Company, 1987
A puzzle book, in which Waldo is hiding in each picture, and the reader must locate him.

Concept Books

Concept books use visuals, sometimes accompanied by text, that help children explore and understand ideas and relationships that are not accessible to them through print alone. Examples include ABC and counting books, photographs that reveal hidden objects, and books which demonstrate size, shape, and color. These books give children jumping-off points for exploring concepts through observation, and dialoguing with adults in a shared-experience situation.

ACTION ALPHABET
Marty Neumeier and Bryon Glaser
Greenwillow Books, 1984
The letters of the alphabet appear as parts of pictures representing words, such as a drip formed by a D coming out of a faucet and a vampire with V's for fangs.

ANNO'S COUNTING BOOK
Mitsumasa Anno
Thomas Y. Crowell, 1977
All the number relationships are shown in natural situations of daily living. As the buildings in the village increase so do the groups and sets of children, adults, trees, boats, and so on.
OTHER BOOKS: *Anno's Alphabet; Anno's Flea Market; Anno's Magical ABC; Anno's Animals; Anno's Mysterious Multiplying Jar; Anno's Hat Tricks.*

ASTER AARDVARK'S ALPHABET ADVENTURES
Steven Kellogg
Morrow Junior Books, 1987
Aster Aardvark didn't like the alphabet, so aunt Agnes decided to change his mind.
OTHER BOOKS: *A My Name is Alice*

CDB
William Steig
Windmill Books, 1968
A puzzle book where the sound of letters represent words, and the pictures give clues as to the meaning.
SEQUEL: *CDC*

CHICKEN SOUP WITH RICE
Maurice Sendak
Scholastic, 1962
Each rhyming verse begins with the name of a month and ends with doing something to the soup, such as blowing it or sipping it.

FIND THE ANIMAL A-B-C
Demi
Grosset and Dunlap, 1985
Readers will have fun playing Demi's find-the-animal game all through this alphabet book.

THE GROUCHY LADYBUG
Eric Carle
Thomas Y. Crowell, 1977
The Grouchy Ladybug thought it was bigger and more important than anyone else and was always ready to pick a fight. But it eventually becomes a happier and slightly better-behaved bug.
OTHER BOOKS: *The Tiny Seed; The Mixed-up Chameleon; All Around Us; The Very Hungry Caterpillar; Do You Want to Be My Friend?; The Secret Birthday Message.*

I CAN BLINK
Frank Asch
Kids Can Press, 1985
Readers can put themselves into the hole of this book and blink like an owl, sniff like a dog, or snap like a turtle.
OTHER BOOKS: *I Can Roar; Happy Birthday, Moon; Moongame; Skyfire.*

THE JOLLY POSTMAN
Janet and Allan Ahlberg
William Heinemann, 1986
This book includes mail received by well-known fairy tale characters, each letter in its own envelope.
OTHER BOOKS: *Each Peach Pear Plum; Funnybones; Peepo!*

THE LOOK AGAIN . . . AND AGAIN, AND AGAIN AND AGAIN BOOK
Beau Gardner
Lee & Shepard, 1984
By turning the book four different ways, the reader may view familiar objects and gain a different perception each time.
OTHER BOOKS: *The Turn About, Think About, Look About Book; The Upside Down Riddle Book.*

ONE WATERMELON SEED
Celia Barker Lottridge; ill. Karen Patkau
Oxford University Press, 1986
This counting book takes a child from one watermelon seed, planted in an empty spring garden, to thousands of puffs of popcorn popped on a winter night. There is opportunity for counting from 1 to 10 as the garden is planted and from 10 to 100 as the harvest is gathered.

OX-CART MAN
Donald Hall; ill. Barbara Cooney
Puffin, 1983
Describes the day-to-day life of an early nineteenth century New England family throughout the changing seasons. Winner of the Caldecott Medal.

Q IS FOR DUCK
Mary Elting & Michael Folsom; ill. Jack Kent
Clarion Books, 1980
A is for Zoo because animals live in the zoo. Children can learn the alphabet along with some facts about animals in this humorous book.

Themes

Themes draw together all types of books by various authors and illustrators into a frame which allows a deeper understanding. As children experience and explore the different perceptions that are found in each book, they have opportunities to draw their own conclusions about which ones they prefer, to begin building a set of patterns about the content and the style of presentation, and to compare and contrast the different facets found within the theme. By collecting books on a particular topic, adults expand the horizons of children, and present opportunities for shared discovery with children of differing print abilities and interests.

Themes: Family and Friends

A BABY SISTER FOR FRANCES
Russell Hoban; ill. Lillian Hoban
Harper Trophy, 1976
Continuing with the Frances series, Frances is back with a younger sister. But Frances isn't sure she wants her in the family.
SERIES: *Bread and Jam for Frances; Bedtime For Frances; Best Friends For Frances; A Birthday for Frances.*

CARROT CAKE
Nonny Hogrogian
Greenwillow Books, 1977
Mr. and Mrs. Rabbit arrive home after their wedding. Trouble begins when the couple has to learn about each other.
OTHER BOOKS: *Noah's Ark; The Devil with the Three Golden Hairs; One Fine Day; The Glass Mountain.*

GORILLA
Anthony Browne
Julia MacRae Books, 1983
More than anything else in the world, Hannah wants to see a live gorilla at the zoo. Her busy father never has time to take her there, so he gives her a toy gorilla for her birthday.
OTHER BOOKS: *Bear Hunt; Piggybook; Willy the Wimp; Willy the Champ; A Walk in the Park; Bear Goes to Town.*

JOHN BROWN, ROSE AND THE MIDNIGHT CAT
Jenny Wagner; ill. Ron Brooks
Puffin, 1980
The story of a special relationship between a widow and her dog,
which is threatened when Rose sees a cat in the garden.
OTHER BOOKS: *The Bunyip of Berkeley's Creek; The Machine at the Heart
of the World.*

MY BROTHER SEAN
Petronella Breinburg; ill. Errol Lloyd
Picture Puffins, 1977
A little boy feels very uncertain on his first day at nursery school.
SERIES: *Sean's Red Bike; Sally-Ann's Umbrella; Sally-Ann in the Snow.*

THE REAL HOLE
Beverly Cleary; ill. DyAnne DiSalvo-Ryan
William Morrow & Company, 1960
Jimmy digs a big hole in the backyard and every one in the family
has a suggestion about what could be done with it.
OTHER BOOKS: *The Growing up Feet; Janet's Thingamajig.*

THE RELATIVES CAME
Cynthia Rylant; ill. Stephen Gammell
Bradbury Press, 1985
A big crowd of all shapes and sizes piled out of an old station
wagon at their relatives' home in the mountains, where they stayed
for weeks.
OTHER BOOKS: *When I Was Young In the Mountains*

WE ARE BEST FRIENDS
Aliki
Greenwillow Books, 1982
Robert is hurt and disappointed when he learns that his best friend
Peter is moving away. Robert's feelings change when he meets Will
and learns that friendship doesn't have to end when a friend moves
away.

WILFRID GORDON MCDONALD PARTRIDGE
Mem Fox; ill. Julie Vivas
Kane/Miller Book Publishers, 1985
A small boy tries to discover the meaning of "memory" so he can
restore that of an elderly friend.

Themes: Humor

ALEXANDER AND THE TERRIBLE, HORRIBLE, NO GOOD, VERY
BAD DAY
Judith Viorst; ill. Ray Cruz
McClelland & Stewart; 1972
Nothing at all went right for Alexander the day he woke up with
gum in his hair.
OTHER BOOKS: *Rosie and Michael; Alexander Who Used to Be Rich Last
Sunday.*

ANIMALS SHOULD DEFINITELY NOT WEAR CLOTHING
Judi Barrett; ill. Ron Barrett
Picture Puffins, 1978
This book is full of the troubles that animals might get into if they
wore clothing.
OTHER BOOKS: *Animals Should Definitely Not Act Like People*

ARTHUR GOES TO CAMP
Marc Brown
Little, Brown & Company, 1982
Arthur isn't looking forward to going to Camp Meadowcroak. When
mysterious things start happening there, he decides to run away.
OTHER BOOKS: *Arthur's Nose; Arthur's Eyes; Arthur's Valentine; Arthur's
Christmas; Arthur's Halloween; Arthur's April Fool; Arthur's
Thanksgiving; Arthur's Tooth; Arthur's Teacher Trouble.*

THE DAY THE TEACHER WENT BANANAS
James Howe; ill. Lillian Hoban
Viking Kestrel, 1984
The new teacher that came to school wasn't what anyone had
expected. He grunted a lot, taught his students to count on their
toes, and ate sixteen bananas for lunch.

I WAS A SECOND GRADE WEREWOLF
Daniel Pinkwater
E.P. Dutton Books, 1983
Lawrence is an average second grade boy until he turns into a
werewolf.
OTHER BOOKS: *Roger's Umbrella; The Moosepire; The Muffin Fiend; The
Frankenbagel Monster.*

JILLIAN JIGGS
Phoebe Gilman
Scholastic-TAB, 1985
Jillian energetically rushes from game to game. One minute she's a robot, the next minute she's a tree. She can never find time to clean up her room when there are so many things to make and do.
OTHER BOOKS: *The Balloon Tree*

MEANWHILE BACK AT THE RANCH
Trinka Hakes Noble; ill. Tony Ross
Dial Books, 1987
Looking for diversion, a bored rancher drives to the town of Sleepy Gulch, little knowing that amazing things are happening to his wife and ranch during his absence.

METEOR!
Patricia Polacco
Dodd, Mead & Company, 1987
A quiet rural community is dramatically changed when a meteor crashes down in the front yard of the Gaw family.

THE PAPER BAG PRINCESS
Robert N. Munsch; ill. Michael Martchenko
Annick Press, 1982
In this modern fairy tale Princess Elizabeth rescues her fiancé Prince Ronald from a fierce dragon. But Ronald is shocked by her untidy appearance and she realizes that he is not the one for her.
OTHER BOOKS: *I Have To Go; Thomas' Snowsuit; The Boy In the Drawer; David's Father; The Mud Puddle; Mortimer; The Dark; Murmel, Murmel, Murmel; 50 Below Zero; Millicent and the Wind.*

THE PIRATE WHO TRIED TO CAPTURE THE MOON
Dennis Haseley; ill. Sue Truesdell
Harper & Row Publishers, 1983
A fierce pirate who lives alone on an island decides to capture all the things that the moon wants and loves in order to take the moon into his posession.

Themes: Adventure

BEAST
Susan Meddaugh
Houghton Mifflin, 1981
The beast came out of the forest. It was big, ugly, and tricky. Anna, who saw it first, decided to find out for herself what the beast was really like.

CLOUDY WITH A CHANCE OF MEATBALLS
Judi Barrett; ill. Ron Barrett
McClelland & Stewart, 1978
Life was delicious in the town of Chewandswallow where it rains soup, snows mashed potatoes, and storms hamburgers—until the weather took a turn for the worse.
OTHER BOOKS: *Old MacDonald Had An Apartment House*

DO NOT OPEN
Brinton Turkle
E.P. Dutton Books, 1981
When Miss Moody opens the mysterious bottle she finds on the beach—which is plainly marked DO NOT OPEN—a remarkable genie comes to life.
OTHER BOOKS: *Obadiah the Bold; Rachel & Obadiah; Deep in the Forest.*

GEORGE SHRINKS
William Joyce
Harper & Row Publishers, 1985
George wakes up one morning to find himself shrunk to the size of a mouse. He also finds a note left by his parents instructing him to do his chores, which he tackles with clever and humorous results.

HAUNTED HOUSE
Jan Pienkowski
E.P. Dutton Books, 1979
This pop-up book shows each room with its own horrors: a flying bat, a snapping crocodile, and an invading alien creature.
OTHER BOOKS: *Little Monsters; Robot; Dinner Time; Gossip.*

HEY, AL
Arthur Yorinks; ill. Richard Egielski
William Collins Sons, 1986
When Al, a janitor, and his faithful dog, Eddie, are transported by a mysterious bird to an island in the sky, they begin a life of ease and comfort. But they soon discover that the grass can be a little too green on the other side. Winner of the Caldecott Medal.
OTHER BOOKS: *Sid and Sol; Louis the Fish; It Happened in Pinsk.*

HILDILID'S NIGHT'
Cheli Durán Ryan; ill. Anita Lobel
Macmillan, 1971
Hildilid hates the night. She thinks that if she can chase away the night, the sun will always shine on her home. A Caldecott Honor Book.

HOT PURSUIT
Kees Moerbeek and Carla Dijs
Price/Stern/Sloan Publishers, 1987
The reader can find out who's chasing whom in this forward-and-backward pop-up book.

THE PATCHWORK CAT
William Mayne; ill. Nicola Bayley
Jonathan Cape, 1981
Tabby loves her patchwork quilt. When she finds it in the garbage can, she settles down for a nap and gets hauled off to the dump, where she spends a terrifying night defending her quilt from rats.

THE RUNAWAY DUCK
David Lyon
Lothrop, Lee & Shepard, 1985
Sebastian's pull-toy duck, Egbert, has many adventures after Sebastian ties him to the bumper of his father's car.

THE TOY CIRCUS
Jan Wahl; ill. Tim Bowers
Harcourt Brace Jovanovich, 1986
A nighttime circus comes to life from a box in a young child's room as the dreaming child becomes the ringmaster.

Themes: Animals and Nature

CHESTER'S BARN
Lindee Climo
Tundra Books, 1982
Everyday life on the farm is portrayed, and the animals come to life
in this introduction to farms. Winner of the 1983 Amelia Frances
Howard-Gibbon Illustrator's Award.

CROW BOY
Taro Yashima
Viking, 1955
A small boy's fear and loneliness at a new school are remarkably
evoked by Yashima's crayon drawings. A sensitive teacher finds the
boy's special talent—imitating the different sounds of crows—and
helps him share it with his classmates.
OTHER BOOKS: *Umbrella; The Village Tree.*

FARM MORNING
David McPhail
Harcourt Brace Jovanovich, 1985
A special relationship between father and daughter is revealed as the
two set out together to feed the farm animals.
OTHER BOOKS: *Sisters*

HATTIE AND THE FOX
Mem Fox; ill; Patricia Mullins
Bradbury Press, 1987
Hattie the hen spots danger but the goose, the pig, the sheep, the
horse, and the cow don't seem to care.
OTHER BOOKS: *Sail Away*

KOKO'S KITTEN
Dr. Francine Patterson; ill. Dr. Ronald H. Cohn
Scholastic, 1985
In 1972, Dr. Francine Patterson began to teach a female gorilla
named Koko how to communicate using the hand and body gestures
of American Sign Language.
SEQUEL: *Koko's Story*

THE NEW BABY CALF
Edith Newlin Chase; ill. Barbara Reid
Scholastic-TAB, 1984
A loving mother knows that baby calves need care, love, and confidence.

A REGULAR ROLLING NOAH
George Ella Lyon; ill. Stephen Gammell
Bradbury Press, 1986
Young Noah tells about loading up the Creeches' whole farm in Kentucky, his first sight of the train, leaving the mountains and drawing up to the flatlands, his job in the boxcar, caring for the animals, and riding the train home again, alone but paid and proud.
OTHER BOOKS: *Father Time and the Day Boxes*

SAM WHO NEVER FORGETS
Eve Rice
Greenwillow Books, 1977
Every day at three o'clock, zookeeper Sam brings his wagon to feed the animals. One day, however his wagon is empty and the elephant hasn't had his food.
OTHER BOOKS: *Benny Bakes A Cake; Goodnight Goodnight; Oh, Lewis!*

SARAH'S QUESTIONS
Harriet Ziefert; ill. Susan Bonners
Lothrop, Lee & Shepard, 1986
The reader may play "I Spy" along with Sarah and her mother as Sarah asks questions about objects she sees on a summer's day.

UP NORTH IN WINTER
Deborah Hartley; ill. Lydia Dabcovich
E.P. Dutton Books, 1986
One icy cold night Grandpa missed the last train home. What happened to him on his long walk back fills this story with a sense of family history and rural roots.

FLOSSIE AND THE FOX
Patricia McKissak; ill. Rachel Isadora
Dial Books, 1986
A young girl meets a sly fox and manages to outwit him.

Themes: Dinosaurs

A BRONTOSAUR
Beverly and Jenny Halstead
William Collins Sons, 1982
This book tells how a brontosaur might have lived his life: what
happened when he hatched from the egg, how big he grew to be,
the dangers he encountered, how he became leader of the herd, and
how eventually his leadership was challenged by a younger
brontosaur.

THE BRONTOSAURUS BIRTHDAY CAKE
Robert McCrum; ill. Michael Foreman
Magnet, 1985
Bobby likes monsters so much, when he cuts his birthday cake
shaped like a brontosaurus, he makes a wish that the creature were
real.

DANNY AND THE DINOSAUR
Syd Hoff
Harper & Row Publishers, 1958
When Danny visited the dinosaur room in the museum, he never
dreamed the dinosaur would talk to him. Or that they would leave
the museum together, with Danny on the dinosaur's back.

DINOSAUR COUSINS?
Bernard Most
Harcourt Brace Jovanovich, 1987
Words and pictures bring out the remarkable similarities between
animals of today and dinosaurs of yesterday.
OTHER BOOKS: *If the Dinosaurs Came Back*

DINOSAURS ARE DIFFERENT
Aliki
Harper Trophy, 1985
Readers can gain valuable information from the skeletons and
reconstructions of prehistoric beasts presented in this book.
OTHER BOOKS: *Digging Up Dinosaurs; Fossils Tell Of Long Ago; My Visit
to the Dinosaurs; Wild and Wooly Mammoths.*

DINOSAURS BEWARE!
Marc Brown and Stephen Krensky
Little, Brown & Company, 1982
These 60 safety tips are illustrated by dinosaurs, usually undergoing the consequences of their actions.

JACOB TWO-TWO AND THE DINOSAUR
Mordecai Richler; ill. Norman Eyolfson
McClelland & Stewart, 1987
Jacob Two-Two is given a dinosaur for a pet but when Dippy grows bigger and bigger he begins to attract attention and ends up on the run from the Canadian government.
SEQUEL: *Jacob Two-Two and the Hooded Fang*

LONG NECK AND THUNDER FOOT
Helen Piers; ill. Michael Foreman
Picture Puffins, 1984
A battle between two prehistoric creatures evolves into a friendship.

TERRIBLE TYRANNOSAURUS
Elizabeth Charlton; ill. Andrew Glass
E.P. Dutton Books, 1986
Pretending to be a tyrannosaurus rex, Nicholas frightens his sister and parents.

WHAT HAPPENED TO PATRICK'S DINOSAURS?
Carol Carrick; ill. Donald Carrick
Clarion Books, 1986
In this sequel to *Patrick's Dinosaurs* young readers, like Patrick, may come to believe that dinosaurs exist in space, watching over the planet earth.
SEQUEL: *Patrick's Dinosaurs*

Read Aloud/Tell Aloud

The oral tradition lives in stories that adults read and tell to children. The strong narrative line draws children into the experience and helps them along the story journey. Since they are hearing the narrative, they are able to understand words, ideas, customs, and values that lie outside their reading abilities. Sharing stories with children allows them to enter worlds past, present, and future, to experience life through the ear, and to absorb print in an interesting and non-threatening manner. Listening to stories read and told aloud gives children their future strength in reading.

BADGER'S PARTING GIFTS
Susan Varley
Lothrop, Lee & Shepard, 1984
At first, those who loved Badger felt overwhelmed by his death. In time though, whenever Badger's name was mentioned, someone would recall something about him that made them all smile.

FLY BY NIGHT
Randall Jarrell; ill. Maurice Sendak
Farrar, Straus & Giroux, 1976
The story of David, who is like other boys during the day but goes on flying excursions at night.
OTHER BOOKS: *The Animal Family*

THE GHOST-EYE TREE
Bill Martin Jr. and John Archambault; ill. Ted Rand
Holt Rinehart & Winston, 1985
Walking down a dark road on an errand one night, a brother and sister argue over who is afraid of the Ghost-Eye tree.
OTHER BOOKS: *White Dynamite and Curly the Kid; Barn Dance.*

HOW TOM BEAT CAPTAIN NAJORK AND HIS HIRED SPORTSMEN
Russell Hoban; ill. Quentin Blake
Macmillan, 1974
Aunt Fidget Wonkhamstrong invites the spirited sportsmen to tackle her rambunctious nephew Tom.

THE HUNDRED DRESSES
Eleanor Estes; ill. Louis Slobodkin
Harcourt Brace Jovanovich, 1944
An outsider joins the class and Maddie reluctantly becomes one of those who tease her. It is not until Wanda moves away that Maddie's conscience bothers her.
OTHER BOOKS: *The Middle Moffat; The Moffats; Rufus M.*

I'M ONLY AFRAID OF THE DARK (AT NIGHT!!)
Patti Stren
Harper & Row Publishers, 1982
Harold, a smart little owl, is afraid of the dark and Gert, his best friend, has a plan to help Harold with his problem.
OTHER BOOKS: *Mountain Rose; Hug Me; There's A Rainbow in My Closet; Sloan and Philamina; The Constrictor That Couldn't.*

JAKE AND HONEYBUNCH GO TO HEAVEN
Margot Zemach
Farrar, Straus & Giroux, 1982
When Jake and his mule, Honeybunch, are struck by a train they are sent straight to heaven where they are overcome by the sight of The Pearly Gates, the Green Pastures, and God himself.
OTHER BOOKS: *Duffy and the Devil; It Could Always Be Worse; To Hilda for helping.*

MAMA DON'T ALLOW
Thatcher Hurd
Harper & Row Publishers, 1984
The Swamp Band has a great time playing loud music until their audience of alligators decides to add them to the menu.
OTHER BOOKS: *The Pea Patch Kid*

MISS EMILY AND THE BIRD OF MAKE-BELIEVE
Charles Keeping
Hutchinson Publishing Group, 1978
Miss Emily buys a beautiful bird from a street vendor, only to find that its colors wash off.
OTHER BOOKS: *Joseph's Yard; Alfie and the Ferry Boat; The Garden Shed; Through the Window.*

THE TAILYPO
Joanne Galdone; ill. Paul Galdone
Clarion Books, 1977
The old man thought someone came into his house, then as he lay still he heard a low voice say, "Tailypo, tailypo, I'm coming to get my tailypo."

TALES OF A GAMBLING GRANDMA
Dayal Kaur Khalsa
Tundra Books, 1986
Reminiscences of a grandmother from Russia who formed a strong bond with her young granddaughter.

THE TERRIBLE THINGS
Eve Bunting; ill. Stephen Gammell
Harper & Row Publishers, 1980
The Terrible Things return again and again to disturb the peacefulness of the forest clearing. Little Rabbit and his animal friends must stand together to overcome the takeover.
OTHER BOOKS: *Magic and the Night River; The Big Cheese; The Man Who Called Down Owls.*

WHY MOSQUITOES BUZZ IN PEOPLE'S EARS
Verna Aardema; ill. Leo and Diane Dillon
Pied Piper, 1978
In this cumulative story, the mosquito tells the iguana a tall tale that sets off a chain reaction for baby owl. Winner of the Caldecott Award.
OTHER BOOKS: *Who's in Rabbit's House; Tales from the Story Hat; What's So Funny, Ketu?; Bimwili and the Zimwi; Bringing the Rain to Kapiti Plain.*

Traditional Tales

Traditional tales cover a wide range of children's literature, from nursery tales told aloud for generations, to authored stories in the folktale tradition. Included in this category are folktales, legends, myths, and fairy tales. They are the legacy of centuries of oral tradition. Children can hear versions from different countries, retold by the Brothers Grimm, Isaac Bachevis Singer, etc. Whether the tales are told or read aloud, child and adult can come together to relive universal truths and experiences.

FOOLISH RABBIT'S BIG MISTAKE
Rafe Martin; ill. Ed Young
G.P. Putnam's Sons, 1985
A little rabbit thinks the earth is breaking up and warns all the animals of the forest. It takes the brave lion's common sense to figure out the foolish rabbit's mistake, and to show the animals how jumping to conclusions can lead to trouble. A retelling of a well-known Jakata tale.

HOW RABBIT STOLE THE FIRE
Joanna Troughton
Blackie & Son, 1979
A North American Indian folk tale about a wily rabbit tricking the
Sky People, and with the aid of his fine feathered headdress,
bringing fire to the animals.
OTHER BOOKS: *Who Will Be the Sun?*; *Mouse-Deer's Market*.

JACK THE GIANT-KILLER
retold by Beatrice Schenk de Regniers, ill. Anne Wilsdorf
Atheneum, 1987
In whimsical verse, de Regniers retells the familiar story of Jack the
Giant-Killer in his first and finest adventure.

LOUHI: WITCH OF NORTH FARM
retold by Toni de Gerez; ill. Barbara Cooney
Viking Kestrel, 1986
The Witch of North Farm has stolen the sun and the moon and
locked them away behind nine great doors in Copper Mountain.
Now darkness is everywhere, and Vainamoinen, the Great Knower,
has plans of his own to deal with the troublesome witch.

THE OLD WOMAN AND THE WILLY NILLY MAN
Jill Wright; ill. Glen Rounds
G.P. Putnam's Sons, 1987
The Willy Nilly Man is a scary old witch man who lives in a shack in
the woods. Not far away lives an old woman, whose shoes dance
and sing uncontrollably at night. When she realizes she cannot go
another night without sleep, she turns to the Willy Nilly Man for
help.

PECOS BILL
Steven Kellogg
William Morrow & Company, 1986
The exploits of Pecos Bill, super-hero of Texas and the Western
pioneers. Like Bill's adventures, the pictures can't be contained by
their frames, making for a spillover of longhorns, rattlesnake-lassos,
and other creatures.
OTHER BOOKS: *Paul Bunyan*

SNOW WHITE
Brothers Grimm; translated by Paul Heins; ill. Trina Schart Hyman
Little, Brown & Company, 1974
Hyman's illustrations for this retelling of Snow White powerfully
express the conflict between good and evil.

STONE SOUP
Marcia Brown
Aladdin, 1986
When three hungry soldiers come to a town where all the food has been hidden, they set out to make soup of water and stones and all the town enjoys a feast. A Caldecott Honor Book.
OTHER BOOKS: *Cinderella; Dick Whittington and his Cat; Shadow; All Butterflies.*

THE TERRIBLE NUNG GWAMA
adapted by Ed Young from the retelling by Leslie Bonnet
William Collins Sons, 1978
A retelling of the Chinese tale in which a poor young woman outwits the terrible monster, Nung Gwama, before he eats her.

VODNIK
Stepan Zaurel
Abelard-Schuman, 1970
A monster called Vodnik dwelt in a lake. Vodnik loved Manya, but Manya was betrothed to Honza, a boy from a nearby village.

Collections

Collections include selections which need not be read in any particular order. They may be written by one author, or selected randomly or themed by an editor. They may include stories, poems, little essays, riddles, and jokes. They can follow different patterns, such as selections for the seasons, or have a linking narration. Often an author simply chooses his or her favorites and builds them into a collection. Children can envelop themselves in a particular genre, such as the Andrew Lang Color fairy tales, or move into a critical frame as they recognize those selections that appealed to them the most within an edited anthology.

FREDERICK'S FABLES
edited by Leo Lionni
Pantheon, 1985
In one volume are thirteen picture books of animal fables. Their texts are unabridged, and the illustrations, which appear on every page, have been carefully selected from the original books.

HUMBLEPUPPY AND OTHER STORIES FOR TELLING
edited by Eileen Colwell
Bodley Head, 1978
There are funny stories, sad stories, retellings of myths and folktales, and also several poems in this collection.
OTHER BOOKS: *More Stories to Tell; A Storyteller's Choice; A Second Storyteller's Choice; The Magic Umbrella.*

THE NEW GOLDEN LAND ANTHOLOGY
edited by Judith Elkin
Puffin, 1984
Not only traditional stories, tall stories, and tongue-twisters, but new stories, nonsense poems, nasty tales, rhymes and riddles, and songs and stories of the supernatural complete this anthology.

THE SECOND MARGARET MAHY STORY BOOK
Margaret Mahy
J.M. Dent & Sons, 1973
A medley of bird-children, kind wizards, kings in broom cupboards, butterflies, goats, kites, and woodland creatures make up another collection of stories and poems by Mahy.
SERIES: *The First Margaret Mahy Story Book; The Third Margaret Mahy Story Book.*
OTHER BOOKS: *The Pirate Uncle; The Bus Under the Leaves; Clancy's Cabin; A Lion in the Meadow and Five Other Favourites.*

THE SPIDER'S PALACE
Richard Hughes
Puffin, 1931
A collection of Hughes's extraordinary and alarming stories.
OTHER BOOKS: *The Wonder Dog*

TOMIE DE PAOLA'S FAVORITE NURSERY TALES
Tomie De Paola
G.P. Putnam's Sons, 1986
This volume contains thirty of the artist's favorite folk tales, fables, and poems for the young.

Poetry and Song

Poetry and song build a child's awareness of rhythm and rhyme and bring pattern and shape to print. Adults can sing or read the lines aloud, or share the print with children as they read together. Today, poetry anthologies and song books abound. Children can choose from all types to fill their particular interests. Some of the books are beautifully illustrated while others depend on the strength of the imagination. Authors and song writers select past favorites, often adapting or rewriting them, and use well-known patterns on which to build new ideas and create wonderful new sounds and images to delight children through the ear. The language structure and vocabulary that are embedded in poem and song give word power for future meaning-making with print.

AUNTIE'S KNITTING A BABY
Lois Simmie; ill. Anna Simmie
Wester Producer Prairie Books, 1984
The characters and creatures of a child's world are presented in a humorous collection of short poems.
OTHER BOOKS: *An Armadillo Is Not a Pillow*

DON'T EAT SPIDERS
Robert Heidbreder; ill. Karen Patkau
1985
Heidbreder has developed sound patterns and rhythms that delight children with a sense of silly, scary things.

EARLY IN THE MORNING
Charles Causely, with music by Anthony Castro; ill. Michael Foreman
Viking Kestrel, 1986
These nursery rhymes are a mix of ancient and modern verse which combine to form a heritage linking generations of parents and children. Twenty of the poems have been set to music.
OTHER BOOKS: *The Puffin Book of Magic Verse; Salt-Sea Verse.*

ELEPHANT JAM
Sharon, Lois & Bram
McGraw-Hill Ryerson, 1986
Sharon, Lois & Bram have put together a collection of their best-loved songs, games, and zany things to do with friends and family from their best-selling records, *One Elephant, Deux Elephants*, and *Smorgasbord.*
OTHER BOOKS: *Sharon, Lois and Bram's Mother Goose*

HURRY, HURRY, MARY DEAR! AND OTHER NONSENSE POEMS
N.M. Bodecker
Atheneum, 1978
This collection offers the reader delights in words and in pictures.
OTHER BOOKS: *It's Raining said John Twaining; The Mushroom Centre Disaster; Let's Marry said the Cherry.*

I'D LIKE TO HEAR A FLOWER GROW
Phyllis Halloran; ill. Carol Reynolds
Reading Inc., 1985
A collection of the author's poems inspired by her work with teachers and children.
OTHER BOOKS: *Cat Purrs*

INKY PINKY PONKY
edited by Michael Rosen and Susanna Steele; ill. Dan Jones
Granada Publishing Group, 1982
A collection of children's playground rhymes with contemporary pictures.

NOW WE ARE SIX
A.A. Milne; ill. E.H. Shephard
Dell Publishing Co., 1986
The gentle verses reflect the forever popular qualities of A.A. Milne's writing.
OTHER BOOKS: *When We Were Very Young*

OUT IN THE DARK AND DAYLIGHT
Aileen Fisher; ill. Gail Owens
Harper & Row Publishers, 1980
In this collection of 140 new poems by Fisher, the winner of the 1978 NCTE Award for Poetry for Children, young people will discover ant villages under rocks, rabbits in moonlight, and puddles for feet to splash in.

THE OXFORD BOOK OF CHILDREN'S VERSE IN AMERICA
edited by Donald Hall
Oxford University Press, 1985
In the tradition of Iona and Peter Opie's *Oxford Book of Children's Verse* comes this anthology compiled by the award-winning poet and children's book author. It includes anonymous works, ballads, and recitation pieces, and ranges from the verses of the seventeenth century to the contemporary nonsense verse.

PLEASE MRS. BUTLER
Allan Ahlberg; ill. Fritz Wegner
Puffin, 1983
A collection of the familiar sayings and events of the classroom.

POEMS FOR 7-YEAR-OLDS AND UNDER
edited by Helen Nicoll; ill. Michael Foreman
Kestrel, 1983
This anthology of poetry includes familiar favorites side by side with fresh and contemporary poems.

THE RAFFI SINGABLE SONGBOOK
Raffi
A collection of 51 songs from Raffi's first three records for young children.

RIDE A PURPLE PELICAN
Jack Prelutsky; ill. Garth Williams
Greenwillow Books, 1986
A collection of rhyming chants with imaginative illustrations.
OTHER BOOKS: *Read-Aloud Rhymes*

SAY IT AGAIN, GRANNY!
John Agard; ill. Susanna Gretz
Bodley Head, 1986
Twenty poems based on Caribbean proverbs.
OTHER BOOKS: *I Din Do Nuttin*

SMALL POEMS AGAIN
Valerie Worth; ill. Natalie Babbitt
Farrar, Straus & Giroux, 1986
A treasury of brief lyrics on such simple but remarkable phenomena as the water lily, the telephone pole, the giraffe, the octopus, and the kaleidoscope.
SERIES: *Small Poems; More Small Poems.*

WHO GOES TO THE PARK
Warabé Aska
Tundra Books, 1984
A visit through the splendors of the park and the wonder of the seasons. Illustrations accompanied by rhyming verse are presented in this award-winning picture book.
OTHER BOOKS: *Who Hides in the Park*

YELLOW BUTTER PURPLE JELLY RED JAM BLACK BREAD
Mary Ann Hoberman
Viking Press, 1981
A rhythmic collection of verses.

Information Books

Information books let children enter the world of facts. Their growing minds are eager for books that describe, explain, label, interpret, and define. Until recently, good information books at appropriate reading levels were scarce. Children could appreciate the photographs, pictures, and diagrams in books, but adults were needed to interpret the writing. Today, authors for children are realizing that there is a growing audience for information presented aesthetically and effectively in books geared to the child's abilities and interests. Adults must be wary of books that purport to present facts but have no appeal or artistic merit. Everything a child reads contributes to his or her picture of what a book can offer. Information books must be no exception.

BEING BORN
Sheila Kitzinger
Lennart Nillson, 1986
In a blend of poetic prose and photographs the experience of the nine-month process from conception to birth is re-created for young readers.

THE GLORIOUS FLIGHT
Alice and Martin Provensen
Viking Press, 1983
A biography of the man whose fascination with flying machines produced the Blériot XI, which crossed the English Channel in thirty-seven minutes in the early 1900s. Winner of the Caldecott Medal.

HOW A BOOK IS MADE
Aliki
Greenwillow Press, 1986
Describes the stages in making a book, starting with the writing of the manuscript and the drawing of pictures, and explaining all the technical processes leading to printed and bound copies.
OTHER BOOKS: *A Medieval Feast; Mummies Made In Egypt.*

HOW TO MAKE POP-UPS
Joan Irvine; ill. Barbara Reid
Kids Can Press, 1987
Everyone can learn how to make their own pop-up cards and books with the easy-to-follow instructions in this book.

THE IMPORTANT THING ABOUT
Joy Troth Friedman
Grosset & Dunlap, 1972
A look at some everyday objects such as strings, boxes, chairs, and hats, accompanied by a descriptive list about why such things are important.

IS THERE LIFE IN OUTER SPACE?
Franklyn M. Branley; ill. Don Madden
Harper Trophy, 1986
This book discusses some of the ideas and misconceptions about life in outer space and speculates on the existence of such life in light of recent space explorations.
OTHER BOOKS: *Flash, Crash, Rumble and Roll; Sunshine Makes the Seasons.*

LET'S CELEBRATE
Caroline Parry
Kids Can Press, 1987
This book brings together national holidays, ethnic holidays, seasonal holidays, religious holidays, and local festivals that are celebrated throughout the country. The book includes the origin and significance of each special day and includes folklore, songs, games, crafts, recipes, and science experiments.

LUCKY CHUCK
Beverly Cleary; ill. J. Winslow Higginbottom
William Morrow & Company, 1984
Cleary tells a funny story of a high-spirited boy who learns the importance of safety. Along the way, this book tells everything needed to be known about motorcycles.

MAPS AND GLOBES
Jack Knowlton
Harper Trophy, 1986
A brief history of mapmaking, a simple explanation of how to read maps and globes, and an introduction to the many different kinds of maps.

THE REASON FOR A FLOWER
Ruth Heller
Grosset & Dunlop, 1983
Vivid pictures and clear explanations are presented in this text that explains how and why flowers grow.
OTHER BOOKS: *Plants that Never Bloom*

SUMMER FUN (Original Titles: THE OWL FUN BOOK and OWL'S SUMMER FUN)
Greey de Pencier, 1987
A book full of facts, information, and activities for summer. There are stories and comics to read, puzzles to do, jokes to enjoy, games to play, and science projects to experiment with.

TRAINS
Gail Gibbons
Holiday House, 1987
Examines different kinds of trains, past and present, describing their features and functions.
OTHER BOOKS: *Department Store; Trucks; The Post Office Book.*

WHAT WOULD YOU DO IF . . . ?
Jeanne Ebert; ill. Laurel Porter
Houghton Mifflin, 1985
This book presents a way of preparing children to handle everyday hazards and unusual emergencies. Each page of the book illustrates a different safety problem and poses the question of what the child would do under those circumstances.

Classics

Classics include those books that have stood the test of time, books parents and grandparents recall experiencing when they were young. Often dated, sometimes slightly sexist or racist, they mirror the society from which they grew, and have a place in the print lives of today's children. Interspersed with contemporary books, classics can still give children great pleasure and draw them inside the memories of the adults that share them.

A BEAR CALLED PADDINGTON
Michael Bond; ill. Peggy Fortnum
Houghton Mifflin, 1962
The Brown family first find this amiable animal on a platform at Paddington Station where he has just arrived from "darkest Peru." They take him home to live with them and life is never the same again.
SERIES: *More About Paddington; Paddington Marches On; Paddington at the Zoo; Paddington at Large; Paddington Helps Out; Paddington Takes the Air.*

BLUEBERRIES FOR SAL
Robert McCloskey
Viking, 1948
Three-year-old Sal and her mother go to the pasture to pick blueberries; so do Little Bear and his mother. Sal drops behind to pick and eat her own blueberries; Little Bear goes slowly, too.
OTHER BOOKS: *Make Way for Ducklings; Time of Wonder; One Morning in Maine.*

IN THE NIGHT KITCHEN
Maurice Sendak
Harper & Row Publishers, 1970
Aroused by noises in the night, Mickey falls out of bed, out of his pajamas, down past his sleeping parents, and into the night kitchen, where three Oliver Hardy-like bakers prepare to bake him in a cake.
OTHER BOOKS: *The Nutshell Library: Alligators All Around, Pierre, One Was Johnny, Chicken Soup with Rice; Where the Wild Things Are; The Sign on Rosie's Door; Some Swell Pup; Outside Over There.*

MADELINE
Ludwig Bemelmans
Viking, 1939
In an old house in Paris lived twelve little girls in two straight lines. The smallest one was Madeline.
SERIES: *Madeline's Rescue; Madeline and the Bad Hat; Madeline and the Gypsies; Madeline in London; Madeline's Christmas.*

PIPPI LONGSTOCKING
Astrid Lindgren; ill. Richard Kennedy
Puffin, 1977
Pippi lives competently with her monkey and her horse, and takes control of any situation in which she finds herself.
SERIES: *Pippi Goes Abroad; Pippi Goes On Board; Pippi in the South Seas; Pippi on the Run.*

ROOTABAGA STORIES
Carl Sandburg
1922; many editions
In the Rootabaga country, mothers, fathers, uncles, and aunts tell stories about the Huckabuck Family, the Potato Face Blind Man, Jason Squiff the cistern cleaner, and the White Horse Girl and the Blue Wind Boy.

THE VELVETEEEN RABBIT
Margery Williams; ill. William Nicholson
Simon & Schuster, 1983
This story, with its description of what it means to be real has appeared in many different illustrated versions since its first publication.

WINNIE-THE-POOH
A.A. Milne; ill. Ernest Shepard
Dell Publishing Co., 1970
Winnie-the-Pooh has a great love of honey and a penchant for creating verses about himself and his friends. Pooh gradually becomes secure in the love of his friend Christopher Robin.
OTHER BOOKS: *The House at Pooh Corner; When We Were Very Young.*

Participation Books

When children share a picture book with an adult, they can often participate if the author has used join-in strategies such as repeating a line, including a refrain, or anticipating an answer to a question. Stories and poems that invite children to share in the telling, or retelling, allow the child to add to the meaning and the enjoyment of the experience. Poems, rhythmic stories, and songs, when used as picture books, provide suitable material for participation reading as well as being literary models for beginning literacy.

BOSS FOR A WEEK
Libby Handy; ill. Jack Newnham
Scholastic-TAB, 1982
Carolyn wants to be boss in the house and make all the rules.

BUTTERSCOTCH DREAMS
Sonja Dunn
Pembroke Publishers, 1987
More than 60 original chants explore the magic of friendship, holidays, food, exotic places, and space travel.

A DARK DARK TALE
Ruth Brown
Scholastic, 1981
A mysterious cat leads the reader on a journey through a dark dark house and up some dark dark stairs which lead to other dark dark objects.

JAMBERRY
Bruce Degen
Harper & Row Publishers, 1983
Rhyme for every kind of berry can be found in this book full of word play and pictures.

THE JUDGE
Harve Zemach; ill. Margot Zemach
Farrar, Straus & Giroux, 1969
Zemach's verse tale about a horrible thing that is coming this way.

THE LITTLE OLD LADY WHO WAS NOT AFRAID OF ANYTHING
Linda Williams; ill. Megan Lloyd
Thomas Y. Crowell, 1986
One autumn night on a path near her cottage, the little old lady heard strange noises.

THE NAPPING HOUSE
Audrey Wood; ill. Don Wood
Harcourt Brace Jovanovich, 1984
A cumulative tale about a snoring granny, a dreaming child, and a dozing dog that will both sooth and amuse young readers.
OTHER BOOKS: *Quick as a Cricket; King Bidgood's in the Bathtub.*

ONCE: A LULLABY
bp Nichol
Black Moss Press, 1983
In this little book, Nichol captures those silent moments of a child just before sleep.

ONE BRIGHT MONDAY MORNING
Arline and Joseph Baum
Random House, 1962
In this cumulative story readers learn to count at the same time as learning about the days of the week and the signs of spring.

ONLY THE BEST
Meguido Zola; ill. Valerie Littlewood
Julia Macrae, 1981
The story of a father who searches for the best gift for his new-born, first-born, and only child, and learns an important lesson about giving and loving.

OVERNIGHT AT MARY BLOOM'S
Aliki
Greenwillow Books, 1987
When Mary Bloom says "Come spend the night," the answer must be "yes", because her home is always filled with fun.
SEQUEL: *At Mary Bloom's*

THE REBUS TREASURY
Jean Marzollo; ill. Carol Devine Carson
Dial Books, 1986
A rebus is a picture that is substituted for a word's sound or meaning. In this collection are forty-one favorite songs and rhymes in full-color rebuses.

ROSIE'S WALK
Pat Hutchins
Macmillan, 1971
The classic tale of a hen who takes a country walk, with danger close behind her.
OTHER BOOKS: *Happy Birthday, Sam; Don't Forget the Bacon!; The Doorbell Rang; Good-Night Owl!*

SO MANY CATS!
Beatrice Schenk de Regniers; ill. Ellen Weiss
Clarion Books, 1985
This story shows how easily one cat can turn into twelve. Readers can count the cats and identify each by name.

THERE WAS AN OLD WOMAN
Stephen Wyllie; ill. Maureen Roffey
Harper & Row Publishers, 1985
In this cumulative tale, the lift-the-flap rebuses will delight young readers and strengthen their word recognition skills.

THE WHEELS ON THE BUS
Maryann Kovalski
Kids Can Press, 1987
An illustrated picture book adaptation of the popular song.

WHY THE TIDES EBB AND FLOW
Joan Chase Bowden; ill. Marc Brown
Houghton Mifflin, 1979
A dauntless old woman bargains with the Sky Spirit against the dramatic backdrop of the ocean swirling down and away forever.

WOULD YOU RATHER . . .
John Burningham
Jonathan Cape, 1978
By having a series of interesting choices on each page, the reader
becomes a participant in each of Burningham's situations.

Beginning Books for Reading

With the wealth of children's books today, no child need begin
reading with limited, meaningless, vocabulary-controlled basal
readers. Depending on the experiences of the child, books for the
beginning reader can explore and depict all aspects of life and
language. The more difficult words, such as "stegosaurus" and
"dinosaur" are easily understood when the story gives the child the
necessary context for understanding the print. Beginning books for
young readers cover a wide range: concept books with labels and
lists; short sentences that explain or illuminate the picture; easy read
books, written by fine authors but with a simple vocabulary; and
picture books with a minimal number of lines and words. The most
important factor about giving children beginning books for reading is
that picture books, poems, and stories should be read aloud in a
parallel pattern to what is being read independently. Experiences
outside and inside print will give children the background they will
need to be mature readers. Limiting their growth to only books they
can read would be a grave mistake.

SPOT'S BIRTHDAY PARTY
Eric Hill
Putnam Publishing Group, 1982
Readers will enjoy the peek-a-boo aspects of the entries of Spot the
puppy.
SERIES: *Where's Spot?; Spot's First Christmas; Spot's First Walk; Spot Goes
to the Farm.*

I WISH I COULD FLY
Ron Maris
Greenwillow Books, 1986
Turtle wishes he could fly, dive, climb, and run like other animals,
but then he realizes something he can do that they can't.

BIG BOSS
Anne Rockwell
Aladdin Books, 1975
The story of how a clever frog outwits a tiger and a fox.
OTHER BOOKS: *The Gollywhopper Egg; Honk Honk!; The Night We Slept Outside.*

A PICTURE FOR HAROLD'S ROOM
Crockett Johnson
Harper & Row Publishers, 1960
With one purple crayon, Harold creates a whole world of moonlight and mountains, ocean liners, and fast-flying jets on his bedroom wall. An "I Can Read" Book.
SERIES: *Harold and the Purple Crayon; Harold's ABC; Harold's Circus; Harold's Trip to the Sky.*

SADIE AND THE SNOWMAN
Allen Morgan; ill. Brenda Clark
Kids Can Press, 1985
Sadie is sad when the snowman she has revived after every winter thaw finally melts in the spring. Then Sadie discovers a way to ensure that her special friend will return with the first snowfall of winter.
OTHER BOOKS: *Molly and Mr. Maloney; Christopher and the Elevator Closet.*

THE TEENY TINY WOMAN
Jane O'Connor; ill. R.W. Alley
Random House, 1986
A teeny tiny woman, who puts a teeny tiny bone she finds in a churchyard away in a cupboard before she goes to sleep, is awakened by a voice demanding the return of the bone.

HENRY AND MUDGE
Cynthia Rylant; ill. Sucie Stevenson
Bradbury Press, 1987
Henry, feeling lonely on a street without any other children, finds companionship in a big dog named Mudge.
SERIES: *Henry and Mudge in Puddle Trouble; Henry and Mudge in the Green Time; Henry and Mudge Under the Yellow Moon; Henry and Mudge in the Sparkle Days.*

MEG AND MOG
Helen Nicoll; ill. Jan Pienkowski
Heinemann, 1972
A humorous adventure with a witch and a cat as central characters.
SERIES: *Meg's Egg; Meg On the Moon.*

FUNNYBONES
Janet and Allen Ahlberg
William Heinemann, 1980
Big Skelton, Little Skelton, and the Dog Skelton are the Funnybones who lease the dark, dark cellar on a dark, dark night and head out into the dark, dark streets hoping to find someone to frighten.
OTHER BOOKS: *Peepo; The Jolly Postman; Each Peach Pear Plum; Burglar Bill; Jeremiah in the Dark Wood; The Ha Ha Bonk Book.*

ONE FISH TWO FISH RED FISH BLUE FISH
Dr. Seuss
Beginner Books, 1960
Dr. Seuss's wordplay in several humorous selections, using strong phonic cues.
OTHER BOOKS: *How the Grinch Stole Christmas; And To Think I Saw It on Mulberry Street; The 500 Hats of Bartholomew Cubbins; Bartholomew and the Ooblek; Green Eggs and Ham; Horton Hatches the Egg; Mr. Brown Can Moo, Can You?; The Cat in the Hat; The Lorax.*

IT'S YOUR TURN, ROGER
Susanna Gretz
Bodley Head, 1985
Roger resents when it's his turn to set the supper table. A visit to neighboring apartments brings him some surprises.
SEQUEL: *Roger Takes Charge!*

ARTHUR'S PRIZE READER
Lillian Hoban
Harper & Row Publishers, 1978
Arthur can read and his younger sister, Violet, can't—or so Arthur says. An "I Can Read" Book.
SERIES: *Arthur's Halloween Costume; Arthur's Honey Bear; Arthur's Funny Money; Arthur's Pen Pal; Arthur's Loose Tooth.*

HARRY TAKES A BATH
Harriet Ziefert
Puffin, 1987
Harry wants to be clean, but he wants to play, too. When he takes a bath, trouble quickly follows. A "Hello Reading" book.
OTHER BOOKS: *The Small Potatoes' Busy Beach Day; The Small Potatoes and the Snowball Fight.*

FROG AND TOAD ARE FRIENDS
Arnold Lobel
Harper Trophy, 1979
Five stories about Frog and Toad and their relationship.
SERIES: *Days with Frog and Toad; Frog and Toad All Year; Frog and Toad Together.*
OTHER BOOKS: *Mouse Tales; Owl at Home; Uncle Elephant.*

FOX AT SCHOOL
Edward Marshall; ill. James Marshall
Dial Press, 1983
Fox was going to be the handsome prince in the school play, but he never thought being a star would mean work.
SERIES: *Fox on Wheels; Fox in Love.*

LOST IN THE MUSEUM
Miriam Cohen; ill. Lillian Hoban
Dell Publishing Co., 1979
The first grade is enjoying a trip to the museum until the teacher and the rest of the class get separated from Danny and Jim.
OTHER BOOKS: *Jim's Dog Muffins; When Will I Read?; First Grade Takes a Test; "Be My Valentine!"; No Good in Art; Starring First Grade; Liar, Liar Pants on Fire!*

LITTLE BEAR'S VISIT
Else Holmelund Minerik; ill. Maurice Sendak
Harper & Row Publishers, 1961
Little Bear loved to visit his grandparents. There was always much to do, much to see, and much to eat. An "I Can Read" Book.
SERIES: *Little Bear; A Kiss for Little Bear; Father Bear Comes Home; Little Bear's Friend.*

MCBROOM'S ZOO
Sid Fleischman; ill. Walter Lorraine
Atlantic Monthly Press, 1972
The McBrooms start a zoo with the Sidehill Gouger, Desert

Vamooser, Silver-tailed Teakettler, and other rare animals left behind by a passing tornado.

SERIES: *McBroom Tells a Lie; McBroom and the Beanstalk; McBroom and the Great Race; McBroom's Ghost; McBroom Tells the Truth; McBroom the Rainmaker; McBroom and the Big Wind; McBroom's Ear.*

THE DRINKING GOURD
F.N. Monjo; ill. Fred Brenner
Harper & Row Publishers, 1970
When some runaway slaves hide in the family barn, Tommy learns of the underground railroad, a secret group of people who believe in giving slaves their freedom.
OTHER BOOKS: *Indian Summer*

First Readers

A quiet revolution has been going on in the teaching of reading. Researchers, teachers, and publishers have been realizing that most children go about learning to read much as they learn to do anything else—by attending to what it means to them and how relevant it is to their accumulated life experience. This has led to the criticism of many reading series for their meaninglessness and for not providing the richness which can come with quality reading.

One consequence of this has been a renewed and increased move by teachers and parents to teach reading using "real books"—that is, a variety of trade books culled from libraries, bookstores, and the few educational publishers who sell boxed collections of children's books. Another result has been, of course, the production of books centered around the language and world of children. A third result has been the trend among mainstream publishers towards producing series of books, by the same or different authors/illustrators, and categorizing them into one or more reading levels. These collections, sets, or series of readers are often used in the classroom as supplementary material to the established reader, or they are used alongside and together with children's books.

This section lists some of the best of these reading series and readers, all of which can take their rightful place among the best of the trade books. The next section, Ready to Read Books, extends this listing for older children.

BANGERS & MASH
Paul Groves; ill. Edward MacLachlan
Longman, 1979
Bangers and Mash are two naughty but lovable chimps whose curiosity frequently leads them into amusing situations. These engaging reads are particularly successful with reluctant beginning readers.
SERIES: *Red Nose; Ant Eggs; Mud Cake; Duck in the Box; The Best Duster; In a Jam; Ding Dong Baby; Red Indians and Red Spots; The Bee and the Sea; Wet Paint; Toothday and Birthday; Bikes and Broomsticks; The Hole Story; The Cow and Bull Story.*
OTHER BOOKS: *Hatching is Catching; Jumpers; Tea Break; Bubble Bath; Garden Trouble; Snatch and Grab; The C.P.O.; Sticky Trousers.*

CAT ON THE MAT READERS
Brian Wildsmith
Oxford University Press, 1983
A series of brief, succinct first readers that tell strong stories—some wordless, the others with short sentences full of repetition—with the help of illustrations.
SERIES: *All Fall Down; My Dream; The Apple Bird; The Island; The Nest; Toot Toot; Trunk; What a Tale; Whose Shoes?*

FIRST READ-BY-MYSELF BOOKS
Patti Wolcott
Addison-Wesley, 1975
This author/illustrator uses only as many words as there are fingers on your hand, with good results.
SERIES: *Beware of a Very Hungry Fox; Double-Decker Bus; I'm Going to Juice; Super Sam and the Green Salad; The Cake Story; The Dragon and the Wild Fandango; The Forest Fire; The Marvelous Mud Washing Machine; Tunafish Sandwiches; Where Did That Naughty Little Hamster Go?*

IMPRESSIONS READING SERIES
edited by Jack Booth, David Booth, Willa Pauli and Jo Phenix
Holt, Rhinehart and Winston, 1984
Designed to provide materials and methodology for the teacher to use in creating an active language environment.
SERIES, GRADE 1: *How I Wonder; Catch a Rainbow; When the Wind Blows; Good Morning Sunshine; Fly Away Home.*
SERIES, GRADE 2: *East of the Sun; West of the Moon.*
SERIES, GRADE 3: *Over the Mountain; Under the Sea.*

THE LETTERMEN
Roger Knights
Lettermen Publishing, 1986
The Lettermen get into one adventure after another as they teach the young reader half a dozen key words in a book.
SERIES: *Lettermen Go Boating; Lettermen Go on a Picnic; Lettermen on the Farm; Lettermen Go to a Party; Lettermen Go to School; Lettermen Go to the Circus; Lettermen Go to the Fair; Lettermen Go to the Park; Lettermen Go to the Seaside; Lettermen Go to the Shop; Lettermen in the Garden; Lettermen in the Kitchen.*

LITTLE NIPPERS
edited by Leila Berg
Macmillan, 1975
One of the first of the modern school readers that reflect the real world of children and model the real language of children—still fresh and immediate.
SERIES, SET A: *Doing the Pools; Hospital Day; Knitting; My Brother; Put the Kettle On; That Baby; The Doctor; Well I Never!*
SERIES, SET B: *A Band in the School; Bubu's Street; Conkers; Fishing; Go On, Then; Growlings, In Bed; My Auntie; My Cat; My Tooth; Once Upon a Time; When Dad Felt Bad.*

MONSTER BOOKS
Ellen Blance and Ann Cook
Longman, 1975
A set of lively stories for all monster lovers.
SERIES: *Monster Comes to the City; Monster Looks for a House; Monster Cleans His House; Monster Looks for a Friend; Monster Meets a Lady Monster; Monster and the Magic Umbrella; Monster Goes to the Museum; Monster at School; Monster Has a Party; Monster Goes to the Zoo.*

PAIRED READING STORY BOOKS
Bill Gillham; ill. Tony Ross and others
Methuen, 1985
Humorous illustrated storylines with a powerful concepts—parent and child read the text in unison—with instructions on this technique for bridging the gap between reading to children and children reading for themselves.
SERIES: *Awful Arabella; Bethy Wants a Blue Ice-Cream; Candy's Camel; Dear Monster; Gertie's Goldfish; Last One in Bed; Nobody Likes My Spider; Our Baby Bites; Our Baby Throws Things; Scribble Sam; Spencer's Spaghetti; Who Needs a Haircut?*

RED NOSE READERS
Allan Ahlberg; ill. Colin McNaughton
Walker, 1985
A library of words and pictures to encourage all early readers. The texts range from words and phrases in Red series through to rhymed sentences in the Blue series.
RED SERIES: *Bear's Birthday; Big Bad Pig; Fee Fi Fo Fum; Happy Worm; Help!; Jumping; Make a Face; So Can I.*
YELLOW SERIES: *Crash! Bang! Wallop!; Me and My Friend; Push the Dog; Shirley's Shops.*
BLUE SERIES: *Blow Me Down!; One, Two, Flea!; Tell Us a Story; Look Out for the Seals.*

Ready to Read Books

Ready to read books give young readers an opportunity to sustain their reading over a longer period of time. Whether the book is a series of short stories about the same characters, or a series of sequential chapters that create a complete story, the books give children the chance to anticipate and predict—the major thinking operations in reading. As the incidents and images grow one upon the other, children build a larger framework for understanding, and may come to realize the pleasure and satisfaction that comes from "a longer read."

AMELIA BEDELIA AND THE BABY
Peggy Parish; ill. Lynn Sweat
William Morrow & Company, 1977
The reader follows Amelia Bedelia through a day as a babysitter, her misinterpretations, and her child care instructions.
SERIES: *Amelia Bedelia; Amelia Bedelia and the Surprise Shower; Amelia Bedelia Goes Camping; Amelia Bedelia Goes Shopping; Amelia Bedelia Helps Out; Come Back, Amelia Bedelia; Good Work, Amelia Bedelia; Play Ball, Amedlia Bedelia; Teach Us, Amelia Bedelia; Thank You, Amelia Bedelia.*

GEORGE AND MARTHA RISE AND SHINE
James Marshall
Houghton Mifflin, 1976
George and Martha, a hippo couple, tame snakes, watch scary movies, and plan surprises.
SERIES: *George and Martha Encore; George and Martha Tons of Fun; George and Martha Back in Town.*

THE STUPIDS DIE
Harry Allard; ill. James Marshall
Houghton Mifflin, 1981
When the lights go out because of a power failure, the Stupids are sure they have died. When the lights come on again, they are convinced they are in heaven.
SERIES: *The Stupids Step Out; The Stupids Have A Ball.*

NATE THE GREAT AND THE STICKY CASE
Marjorie Wienman Sharmat; ill. Marc Simont
Dell Publishing Co., 1978
A stegosaurus stamp belonging to Nate's friend Claude disappears, and Nate the Great is called in on the case.
SERIES: *Nate the Great; Nate the Great and the Phony Clue; Nate the Great and the Lost List; Nate the Great Goes Underground; Nate the Great and the Missing Key.*

GUS AND BUSTER WORK THINGS OUT
Andrew Bronin; ill. Cyndy Szekeres
Dell Publishing Co., 1975
Gus uses all his cunning to get the best of Buster, but his schemes have a way of backfiring when the two brother raccoons get together.

ARNOLD OF THE DUCKS
Mordecai Gerstein
Harper & Row Publishers, 1983
Arnold is in his wading pool when a nearsighted pelican suddenly scoops him up in his bill, flies off, and drops him in the middle of some freshly hatched ducklings.

THE FOUNDLING
Carol Carrick; ill. Donald Carrick
Clarion Books, 1977
His parents try to get Christopher another dog, but he is faithful to his dog Bodger, who was killed.
OTHER BOOKS: *Lost in the Storm; Sleep Out; The Accident.*

THE SANDWICH
Ian Wallace and Angela Wood
Kids Can Press, 1975
Vincenzo wants to be just like his friends, but his Italian heritage presents a major roadblock.

STAIRWAY TO DOOM
Robert Quackenbush
Simon & Schuster, 1983
Miss Mallard has been invited to Duckinhill Castle to hear the will of her late great aunt, but the other guests disappear.
SERIES: *Bicycle to Treachery; Cable Car to Catastrophe; Dig to Disaster; Express Train to Trouble; Gondola to Danger; Richshaw to Horror; Stage Door to Terror; Surfboard to Peril; Taxi to Intrigue.*

First Novels

First novels mark a reading plateau for young independent readers because they are now able to sustain their interest over several chapters, making sense of plot and characters as the information builds up, and finding aesthetic pleasure in the wholeness of the longer story. Children may enjoy reading a series of novels by one author, discovering more about familiar characters, or read several novels on a theme, such as mystery or humor. It is important that children not be pushed into reading novels either not interesting to them or too difficult for them, for success in this phase in their reading growth may determine their futures as readers.

PADDINGTON HELPS OUT
Michael Bond
William Collins Sons, 1960
Paddington's adventures take place in seven chapters, and trouble comes naturally to Paddington.
SERIES: *A Bear Called Paddington; More about Paddington; Paddington Abroad; Paddington at Large; Paddington Marches On; Paddington at Work; Paddington Goes to Town; Paddington Takes the Air; Paddington on Top; Paddington Takes the Test; Paddington's Blue Peter Story Book; Paddington on Screen.*

DECEMBER SECRETS
Patricia Reilly Giff
Dell Publishing Co., 1984
It is December, and everyone in the class has a secret friend that they have to be kind to no matter how hard it is. This story is one of the "Kids of the Polk Street School" series.
OTHER BOOKS: *The Beast in Ms. Rooney's Room; Fish Face; The Candy Corn Contest; In the Dinosaur's Paw; The Valentine Star; The Riddle of the Red Purse; The Mystery of the Blue Ring.*

THE CARP IN THE BATHTUB
Barbara Cohen; ill. Joan Halpern
Kar-Ben Copies, 1972
While the whole family is busy preparing for the Passover holidays,
a young brother and sister are determined to save the life of the carp
who's destined to become served for dinner.
OTHER BOOKS: *Molly's Pilgrim; Gooseberries to Oranges; The Secret Grove.*

STORM
Kevin Crossley-Holland
William Heinemann, 1985
One stormy night, Annie is offered a ride by a tall, silent horseman.
She accepts.

DRACULA IS A PAIN IN THE NECK
Elizabeth Levy; ill. Mordecai Gerstein
Harper & Row Publishers, 1983
Strange and frightening things have been happening at Camp
Hunter Creek, and Robert thinks Dracula might be haunting the
area. Robert and his older brother Sam must find out what's going
on.
OTHER BOOKS: *Frankenstein Moved in on the Fourth Floor*

THE SHERLUCK BONES MYSTERY-DETECTIVE BOOKS
Jim and Mary Razzi; ill. Ted Enik
Bantam Books, 1983
A series of books where the readers can find the clues along with
the characters of Bones and Scotson to try to solve a series of
mysteries, crimes, and puzzles.

LOST AND FOUND
Jean Little
Puffin, 1986
Lucy's family moves to a new town where she meets a friendly dog
that may or may not be a stray.

THE COURAGE OF SARAH NOBLE
Alice Dalgleish
Charles Scribner's Sons, 1954
This is the true story of eight-year-old Sarah who accompanies her
father into the wilderness to cook for him while he builds a cabin for
their family. With each adversity, Sarah remembers her mother's
advice to "keep up her courage." A Newbery Honor Book.
OTHER BOOKS: *The Bears on Hemlock Mountain*

BE A PERFECT PERSON IN JUST THREE DAYS
Stephen Manes
Bantam Books, 1983
One day a book entitled "Be A Perfect Person in Just Three Days"
falls on Milo's head and Milo decides to become a perfect person,
even if it means wearing broccoli around his neck for twenty-four
hours.
OTHER BOOKS: *The Boy Who Turned Into a TV Set; The Hoople's Haunted
House.*

JAMES AND THE GIANT PEACH
Roald Dahl
Alfred A. Knopf, 1961
James finds adventure in a giant peach with his friends, a
grasshopper, a ladybug, a spider, a centipede, an earthworm, and a
silkworm.
OTHER BOOKS: *The Twits; George's Marvelous Medicine; Charlie and the
Chocolate Factory; Fantastic Mr. Fox.*

THE VANISHMENT OF THOMAS TULL
Janet and Allan Ahlberg
Puffin, 1985
Thomas Tull stopped growing when he was seven years old, but
when he started shrinking, his parents began to seek ways to restore
their much-loved son to his former size.

THE THREE AND MANY WISHES OF JASON REID
H.J. Hutchins
Annick Press, 1983
Even though Jason knew he wasn't supposed to talk to strangers, he
is delighted to meet eighteen inch Elster of the Third Order who
grants him three wishes. Number one and number two wish can be
accommodated, but for his third wish Jason asks for three more
wishes. That, of course, is against the rules.

THE CRICKET IN TIMES SQUARE
George Selden; ill. Garth Williams
Farrar, Straus & Giroux, 1960
Three friends—a cat, a mouse, and a cricket survive in a newspaper
stand in New York City.
SERIES: *Tucker's Countryside; Harry Kitten and Tucker Mouse.*

The Middle Years

The years between nine and twelve reveal the individualization of both the interests and the abilities of children. The range of reading levels is varied, and tastes shift quickly from day to day. The lives of the children are filled with clubs, lessons, sports, and television, and books can take a back seat without the support of interested adults. Although many readers have reached a level of independence, their listening abilities still outreach their independent reading abilities, and therefore it is still important for them to be read to. The selections in this section include books for sharing as well as books for the developing, reluctant, and independent reader. The pressure of the peer group may determine their reading choices: those children with limited reading success may need a great deal of support from adults to continue growing with books. We have provided suggestions for short, simple books, longer novels, and strong, sophisticated fiction. Thematic suggestions fulfill the needs of these children for a variety of reading preferences, including familiar authors, series, and contemporary topics. As well, there are representative selections from the popular children's choices, classics, and new titles. Some recent information books are included to remind adults of the wide variety of instructional, reference, and non-fiction materials written for this age group. Picture books, folklore, and poetry provide both sources for sharing and for silent reading.

Children can learn about many aspects of life vicariously through books, while having enriching literary experiences. Since good books are forms of art, the perceptions and views built up through literature will give children a strong affective and cognitive basis for life as well as a secure grounding in literacy.

Easy Read Fiction

Children in the middle years represent a great range of reading abilities. Yet their common need is to read widely and often. A large selection of books is necessary for those children who are moving into independent reading, but who may not have much security with print, who need high motivation accompanied by material that is accessible. A child in fourth or fifth grade requires books at his or her interest level while written at a level that the child can handle. A child needs a book with a story in which he can become immersed, so that he or she wants to read it completely and feel the satisfaction and pleasure that a good book gives. Books that are written with a controlled vocabulary but little art will seldom make a child want to continue reading.

POP BOTTLES
Ken Roberts
Douglas & McIntyre, 1987
In Vancouver, 1933, times are difficult for Ray and Willie. Life is fairly uneventful until the boys discover that the walkway in front of Will's new house is made from thousands of pop bottles, and each bottle is worth two cents at the local store.
OTHER BOOKS: *Crazy Ideas*

MAGGIE AND ME
Ted Staunton
Kids Can Press, 1986
A collection of five funny stories starring Cyril and his best friend Maggie, the Greenapple Street Genius. No matter what they do, the two friends seem to get in trouble, then cleverly manage to find their way out of it.
OTHER BOOKS: *Taking Care of Crumley; Greenapple Street Blues.*

THE TWITS
Roald Dahl
Bantam Skylark, 1982
Mr. and Mrs. Twit play the nastiest tricks on each other. She feeds him worms, and he puts frogs in her bed.
OTHER BOOKS: *Charlie and The Chocolate Factory; James and the Giant Peach; Fantastic Mr. Fox; Charlie and the Great Glass Elevator; George's Marvelous Medicine.*

RAMONA THE PEST
Beverly Cleary
Dell Publishing Co., 1965
Life for Ramona is so interesting she always has to find out what will happen next. This is the first in a series of books about Ramona and her humorous experiences.
SERIES: *Ramona Quimby, Age 8; Ramona and Her Mother; Ramona and Her Father; Beezus and Ramona; Ramona the Brave.*
OTHER BOOKS: *Henry Huggins; Henry and the Clubhouse; Otis Spofford; The Mouse and the Motorcycle; Ralph's Mouse; Socks; Ribsy.*

NOTHING'S FAIR IN FIFTH GRADE
Barthe De Clements
Scholastic, 1981
Elsie Edwards is the new girl in her fifth grade class. Not only is she overweight, but she's accused of stealing everyone's lunch money. Jenny Moore is assigned to keep an eye on Elsie and the two girls become fast friends who help each other when things get unfair in the fifth grade.
OTHER BOOKS: *Sixth Grade Can Really Kill You*

HOW TO EAT FRIED WORMS
Thomas Rockwell
Dell Publishing Co., 1973
Because of a bet, Billy must eat fifteen worms in fifteen days. He tries using ketchup, horseradish, and peanut butter. But fifteen worms are a lot to eat.
OTHER BOOKS: *Humph!; The Neon Motorcycle; Squawwwk; The Thief.*

FIFTH GRADE MAGIC
Beatrice Gormley
Avon Camelot, 1984
Gretchen Nichols wanted to star in the school play. When her teacher chose the new girl, pretty blonde Amy Sacher for the starring role, Gretchen was desperate enough to appeal to a strange visitor to help her.
OTHER BOOKS: *Mail-Order Wings; Best Friend Insurance.*

DEAR RAT
Julia Cunningham
Avon Camelot, 1976
Andrew, a rat from Humpton, Wyoming, recently arrived in France. A villainous mobster named Groge schemes to steal the Chartres Cathedral jewels and dispose of them at the Royal Court.
OTHER BOOKS: *Dorp Dead; Flight of the Sparrow; Burnish Me Bright.*

THE TROUBLE WITH THIRTEEN
Betty Miles
Avon Books, 1979
Annie and Rachel wish they could stay twelve forever, but
unexpected changes begin pulling the girls apart just when they
need each other the most.
OTHER BOOKS: *Maudie and Me and the Dirty Book; Sink or Swim; Just the
Beginning; The Real Me; I Would If I Could; The Secret Life of the
Underwear Champ.*

Fiction for Developing Readers

The middle years are the quantity years, when children gain reading
power through in-depth experiences with novels. Many fine books
have been written with this in mind. Children enjoy reading several
books by a favored author or a series of books about a familiar set of
characters. Common themes link the most widely-read books—
humor, school friends, mystery, fantasy—and children should be
given as many opportunities as possible for reading independently.
Boys and girls may prefer different types of books, yet there are fine
novels which, if brought to their attention, will fill their interest
needs and present non-sexist portrayals.

FOURTH GRADE CELEBRITY
Patricia Reilly Giff
Dell Publishing Co., 1979
Casey Valentine is tired of being compared to her popular older
sister and is determined to get herself elected class president.
SERIES: *Left-Handed Shortstop; The Winter Worm Business; The Girl Who
Knew It All.*
OTHER BOOKS: *Have You Seen Hyacinth McCaw?; Loretta P. Sweeny,
Where Are You?; The Gift Of the Pirate Queen.*

THE WHIPPING BOY
Sid Fleischman
Greenwillow Books, 1986
It was forbidden to spank the heir to the throne, so a young orphan
named Jemmy had been plucked from the streets to serve as a
whipping boy to the arrogant and spiteful Prince Brat. Winner of the
1986 Newbery Medal.
OTHER BOOKS: *The Ghost In The Noonday Sun; Bullwhip Griffin; Humbug
Mountain; Chancy and the Grand Rascal; By the Great Horn Spoon.*

THAT SCATTERBRAIN BOOKY
Bernice Thurman Hunter
Scholastic-TAB, 1981
In the Great Depression, Booky was hungry all the time, her parents fought constantly, and the bailiff would soon return to evict her family from their home. Worst of all, she knew that Christmas would be a time of empty stockings instead of presents under the tree.
SERIES: *With Love, From Booky; As Ever, Booky.*
OTHER BOOKS: *Margaret in the Middle; A Place for Margaret.*

SLAKE'S LIMBO
Felice Holman
Dell Publishing Co., 1977
Orphaned thirteen-year-old Aremis Slake took his dreams into the subway system and there he lived beneath the world on his own for one hundred and twenty-one days.
OTHER BOOKS: *The Wild Children; Elisabeth & the Marsh Mystery.*

A STRANGER AT GREEN KNOWE
Lucy Boston
Harcourt Brace Jovanovich, 1979
The miserable creatures of the monkey house depress Ping, a Chinese orphan, until he catches sight of the magnificent gorilla, Hanno. Ping is moved by Hanno's power and rage, and the two develop a close relationship.
SERIES: *The Children of Green Knowe; The Treasure of Green Knowe; An Enemy at Green Knowe; The River at Green Knowe.*
OTHER BOOKS: *The Sea Egg*

VERONICA GANZ
Marilyn Sachs
Scholastic, 1987
Veronica Ganz was a bully, but in little Peter Wedemeyer, she may have met her match.
OTHER BOOKS: *Peter and Veronica; Amy Moves In; Amy and Laura; The Truth About Mary Rose Underdog; A Secret Friend; Fourteen; Dorrie's Book; The Bear's House.*

FANNY AND THE MONSTER
Penelope Lively
Puffin, 1982
Fanny was supposed to be a proper little Victorian girl, but she wanted to be a paleontologist. She slipped away alone to follow a

notice that read: TO THE PREHISTORIC MONSTERS. Then she disappeared.
OTHER BOOKS: *The Revenge of Samuel Stokes; The Ghost of Thomas Kempe; The Voyage of QV66; The Stained Glass Window; A House in Norham Gardens; A Stitch in Time.*

THE DIDDAKOI
Rumer Godden
Penguin, 1977
A half-gypsy child suffers from her own stubbornness as well as from the cruelty of her classmates. The loving care of a spinster, an Admiral, his servants, and eventually the whole village, provide her with a positive new life.
OTHER BOOKS: *Four Dolls; The Dragon of Og; The Valiant Chatti-Maber; The Rocking Horse Secret; The Mouse Wife.*

THE PERSUADING STICK
John Rowe Townsend
Lothrop, 1987
With the help of a magic stick a quiet English girl becomes more and more assertive.
OTHER BOOKS: *Dan Alone; Top of the World; Gumble's Yard.*

THE EGYPT GAME
Zilpha Keatley Snyder
Atheneum, 1972
April and Melanie discover a chipped replica of the famous Nefertiti statue in an overgrown vacant lot behind a junk shop, and begin the Egypt game. The two friends read about ancient Egypt, make costumes, and develop shrines and rituals for their secret world. A Newbery Honor Book.
OTHER BOOKS: *The Headless Cupid; Blair's Nightmare; The Changeling; The Witches of Worm; The Famous Stanley Kidnapping Case.*

CHILDREN OF THE WOLF
Jane Yolen
Viking Press, 1984
A frightened villager tells stories of ghosts in the nearby jungle. The creatures are captured and brought back to the orphanage. They turn out to be not ghosts, but two young girls who have been raised by wolves. Yolen has based her novel on an actual account of feral children in India in the 1920s.
OTHER BOOKS: *The Gift of Sarah Baker; Simple Gifts.*

THE OTHER WAY AROUND
Judith Kerr
Dell Publishing Co., 1979
In this sequel to *When Hitler Stole Pink Rabbit* Anna is a fifteen-year-old German wartime refugee in London, struggling to cope with her alien status, poverty, a typing course, bombing raids, her first job, and first love.
SEQUEL: *When Hitler Stole Pink Rabbit*

Fiction for Independent Readers

For those children who have developed into mature, independent readers in the middle years, many novels are available they will enjoy reading that, while at an appropriate print and emotional level, will also challenge their concepts and ideas. Rather than move to "harder" or more adult fiction, these children need to deepen their reading experiences by moving into quality alongside quantity. Novels from other countries, other cultures, or other contexts can present these young readers with problems and situations of greater complexity, subtle characterization, and multifaceted plot structures. These children can read the novels that represent the best in fiction for children.

HARRIET THE SPY
Louise Fitzhugh
Dell Publishing Co., 1964
Harriet the Spy has a secret notebook that she fills with honest jottings about her parents, her classmates, and her neighbors. Every day on her spy route she "observes" and notes down anything and everything that interests her. But Harriet's notebook is found by her schoolmates.
SEQUELS: *The Long Secret; Sport.*

ZEELY
Virginia Hamilton
Aladdin Books, 1987
Elizabeth spends the summer on Uncle Ross's farm and encounters tall and dignified Zeely Tayber. When the young girl discovers a picture of a Watusi queen she is sure that with Zeely, she is in the presence of royalty.

THE PHANTOM TOLLBOOTH
Norton Juster; ill. Jules Feiffer
Windward Books, 1972
When Milo drove his small electric car through the tollbooth gate, he found himself in The Lands Beyond, home of some of the strangest creatures ever imagined.

BRIDGE TO TERABITHIA
Katherine Paterson; ill. Donna Diamond
Avon Camelot, 1977
It was Leslie's idea to create Terabithia, a secret kingdom in the woods where Leslie and Jesse could reign as King and Queen. Jesse's special friendship with Leslie and the worlds of imagination and learning which she opens up to him enable him to cope with the unexpected tragedy that strikes. A Newbery Award Winner.
OTHER BOOKS: *Come Sing, Jimmy Jo; The Great Gilly Hopkins; Rebels of the Heavenly Kingdom; The Master Puppeteer.*

A FINE WHITE DUST
Cynthia Rylant
Bradbury Press, 1986
Peter narrates falling under the spell of an intense preacher conducting a revival meeting. He becomes a born-again Christian during an emotional service, but in the aftermath has trouble sorting out his feelings. A Newbery Honor Book.

A WRINKLE IN TIME
Madeleine L'Engle
Dell Publishing Co., 1973
On a dark and stormy night, Meg Murry, her small brother Charles Wallace, and her mother were upset by the arrival of a most disturbing stranger who tells the family of a "tesseract", a wrinkle in time. This is the first title in a trilogy and is a Newbery Award Winner.
SEQUELS: *A Wind In The Door; A Swiftly Tilting Planet; Many Waters.*

THE DREAM TIME
Henry Treece
Hodder & Stoughton, 1967
In the dawn of time, when men fought with flint spears, there lived a boy named Crookleg who did not want to be a war-man; he wanted to make pictures. In search of a peace-loving tribe he wandered into the forest, where the girl Blackbird led him, he stayed

with the River Folk and their Headwoman, Wander, and he visited the Red Men, who lived in caves.
OTHER BOOKS: *(Trilogy) Viking's Dawn; The Road to Miklagaard; Viking's Sunset.*

THE MYSTERIOUS DISAPPEARANCE OF LEON (I MEAN NOEL)
Ellen Raskin
Avon Camelot, 1980
Adopted twins Tony and Tina are called upon to help Mrs. Carillon seek her long-lost husband in this mystery adventure.
OTHER BOOKS: *The Westing Game; The Tattooed Potato and Other Clues.*

MRS. FRISBY AND THE RATS OF NIMH
Robert C. O'Brien
Atheneum, 1971
Mrs. Frisby, a widowed mouse with four children, is a heroine faced with the move to winter quarters while Timothy, her youngest child, is very ill. She seeks the help of a wise old owl and through him meets the rats of NIMH, experimental rats who had become highly intelligent and had planned and executed a daring escape from the laboratory. Winner of the Newbery Medal. (Paperback title: *The Secret of NIMH*)
SEQUEL: *Rasco and the Rats of NIMH, by Jane Leslie (daughter of Robert C. O'Brien)*

Themes

Fiction for children in the middle years revolves around several recurring themes—friends, family, fantasy, humor, sports, mystery, adventure, history, nature, and contemporary issues. These universals represent the interests and concerns of pre-adolescents— peer groups, their place in the social system, and the complexity of growing up. Even the most fantastical of novels reveals an underpinning of real situations and problems. For many children, novels provide road maps for the difficulties of contemporary life. They can identify with and live through the exploits of the fictitious characters. Through themes, adults can help provide children with specific concerns via a range of novels that may meet their wants and needs.

Themes: Relationships

THE PINBALLS
Betsy Byars
Scholastic, 1977
Carlie, Harvey, and Thomas J. have all been sent to live with foster parents. Though the three characters meet love and fun for the first time, they'd all rather be back in their own homes.
OTHER BOOKS: *The Cybil War; Cracker Jackson; The Cartoonist; After the Goat Man; The House of Wings; The Midnight Fox; The Night Swimmers; Summer of the Swans; The 18th Emergency; The Computer Nut; The Not-Just-Anybody Family; The Glory Girl.*

A GIRL CALLED AL
Constance C. Greene
Dell Publishing Co., 1978
Two best friends go through the perils of young adolescence.
SERIES: *I Know You, Al; Al(exandra) the Great; Your Old Pal, Al.*
OTHER BOOKS: *Isabelle the Itch; Isabelle Shows Her Stuff; The Ears of Louis; I and Sproggy; The Unmaking of Rabbit; Double-Dare O'Toole.*

ANASTASIA KRUPNIK
Lois Lowry
Bantam Books, 1981
Being ten is very confusing for Anastasia Krupnik. Problems with her teacher, her sixth-grade boyfriend, a grandparent and her mother who is having a baby make Anastasia feel that she might not make it to her eleventh birthday.
SERIES: *Anastasia Again; Anastasia At Your Service; Anastasia, Ask Your Analyst; Anastasia Has The Answer; Anastasia On Her Own.*
OTHER BOOKS: *The One Hundredth Thing About Caroline; Switcharound; Autumn Street.*

DEAR MR. HENSHAW
Beverly Cleary; ill. Paul O. Zelinsky
Dell Publishing Co., 1984
Through the letters he writes to his favorite author, Mr. Henshaw, and through his private journal entries, the reader gets to know sixth grader Leigh Botts, who is confronted with the problems of living without a father, having a lunch stolen, and wanting to become a writer. Winner of the Newbery Award.
OTHER BOOKS: *The Mouse and the Motorcycle; Ramona the Pest; Henry Huggins.*

HEY DAD!
Brian Doyle
Groundwood Books, 1978
Megan's looking forward to spending the summer constructing a clubhouse for the "Down With Boys" Club, something she'd definitely prefer over travelling across the country with her family.
OTHER BOOKS: *Up To Low; Angel Square; You Can Pick Me Up at Peggy's Cove.*

MAMA'S GOING TO BUY YOU A MOCKINGBIRD
Jean Little
Penguin, 1984
This family story is about the changes in a young boy when his father becomes ill and dies.
OTHER BOOKS: *From Anna; Listen For the Singing; Look Through My Window; Kate; Different Dragons.*

ONE-EYED CAT
Paula Fox
Dell Publishing Co., 1985
Ned Wallis is given a rifle for his birthday by his uncle. He is forbidden to touch the rifle until he is older. However, he sneaks it out of the house just once and shoots at a dark shadow. A Newbery Honor Book.
OTHER BOOKS: *How Many Miles To Babylon?; The Slave Dancer; The Moonlight Man; The Stone-faced Boy; Portrait of Ivan; Blowfish Live in the Sea; A Likely Place; Maurice's Room.*

I, TRISSY
Norma Fox Mazer
Laurel Leaf, 1977
Ann loved the new typewriter her father gave her when he left home. "Tris," he said, "now you can put down on paper all the things you're always making the mistake of saying out loud, and nobody has to know them except you." Trissy writes about her problems and about the frustrations of living in a divorced family.
OTHER BOOKS: *A Figure Of Speech; Saturday, The Twelfth of October; Mrs. Fish, Ape, and Me, the Dump Queen.*

DANCING CARL
Gary Paulsen
Puffin, 1987
As winter progresses, the strange man in the worn flight jacket

dances frequently on the ice of the rink, expressing more with his movements than most people do with words.
OTHER BOOKS: *Tracker*

THE FINDING
Nina Bawden
Puffin, 1987
Alex had been found as a baby in the arms of a statue. He'd been famous then, briefly, appearing on television, his photograph in all the papers. Now after eleven years, the publicity is happening to him again, and he's confused about his past and present worlds.
OTHER BOOKS: *Carrie's War; The Peppermint Pig; Squib; The Secret Passage; The Runaway Summer; Rebel on a Rock; The Robbers; A Handful of Thieves; Kept in the Dark.*

Themes: Mystery and Adventure

THE BFG
Roald Dahl
Farrar, Straus & Giroux, 1982
A giant has been lurking on the street, blowing something from a glass jar into children's bedrooms. He sees little Sophie, who has much to learn about the BFG.
OTHER BOOKS: *The Witches; The Magic Finger.*

NICOBOBINUS
Terry Jones; ill. Michael Foreman
Viking Kestrel, 1985
Nicobobinus is an extraordinary child with an extraordinary name, who meets kidnapping pirates, murderous monks, mountains that move, and a ship that can cook.
OTHER BOOKS: *The Saga of Erik the Viking*

HAUNTED HOUSE
Peggy Parish
Dell Publishing Co., 1985
Liza, Bill, and Jed soon realize that something weird is happening in and around their new home since every morning they find mysterious messages.
OTHER BOOKS: *Key to the Treasure; Clues in the Woods; Hermit Dan; Pirate Island Adventure.*

THE FIGURE IN THE SHADOWS
John Bellairs
Dell Publishing Co., 1977
The adventures of Uncle Jonathan Van Olden Baravelt, fat and
friendly warlock, and his kindly witch girlfriend, Mrs. Zimmerman.
OTHER BOOKS: *The House with a Clock in Its Walls; The Revenge of the
Wizard's Ghost; The Spell of the Sorcerer's Skull; The Mummy, the Will
and the Crypt; The Curse of the Blue Figurine; The Letter, the Witch & the
Ring.*

THE MINERVA PROGRAM
Claire Mackay
James Lorimer & Company, 1984
Because of a trick, Minerva finds herself banned from using the
school computers. Her brother "Spiderman" and her inventive
friends devise a scheme to expose the real culprit and solve the
mystery.

DOUBLE SPELL
Janet Lunn
Clarke Irwin, 1968
Two twins search to discover the history of the little doll which
brings them terrifyingly close to the world of the supernatural.

THE TURQUOISE TOAD MYSTERY
Georgess McHargue
Dell Publishing Co., 1983
Ben Pollock is invited by his Aunt Celie to spend Christmas vacation
at an archaelogical dig in Arizona. He heads off into the desert with
his camera, where his curiosity lands him in the middle of a
mystery involving valuable Indian artifacts and a murderous ring of
"pot robbers."
OTHER BOOKS: *Funny Bananas; The Impossible People; Meet the Witches;
The Talking Table Mystery.*

HIDDEN GOLD MYSTERY
Marion Cook
Overlea House, 1987
Megan is preparing her pet pig, Susie, to be shown at a 4-H rally
but when the pig escapes Megan finds herself faced with the
mystery surrounding the death of an old prospector.
OTHER BOOKS: *Payment in Death; Stone Dead.*

THE INDIAN IN THE CUPBOARD
Lynne Reid Banks
Avon Camelot, 1982
A nine-year-old boy receives a plastic Indian, a cupboard, and a little
key for his birthday, then finds himself involved in adventure when
the Indian comes to life in the cupboard and befriends him.
SEQUEL: *The Return of the Indian*

THE VIEW FROM THE CHERRY TREE
Willo Davis Roberts
Macmillan, 1987
Rob tries to tell the police that Mrs. Calloway has been murdered
but the officers don't listen. Neither does his family, who are too
busy preparing for his older sister's wedding.
OTHER BOOKS: *The Pet-Sitting Peril; Don't Hurt Laurie; Eddie and the
Fairy Godpuppy.*

FROM THE MIXED-UP FILES OF MRS. BASIL E. FRANKWEILER
E.L. Konigsburg
Dell Publishing Co., 1977
Claudia runs away from home and takes her brother Jamie along to
finance the expedition. They take up residence in the Metropolitan
Museum of Art and become involved in the search for a sculpture.
OTHER BOOKS: *Up From Jericho Tel; Journey to an 800 Number; Jennifer,
Hecate, Macbeth, William McKinley, and Me, Elizabeth.*

Themes: Issues

IN THE YEAR OF THE BOAR AND JACKIE ROBINSON
Bette Bao Lord
Harper Trophy, 1986
Shirley Temple Wong sails from China to America with a heart full
of dreams to a new home, Brooklyn. Shirley doesn't know any
English, and it's so hard to make friends. Jackie Robinson is
everyone's hero, and proves that a black man can make a difference
in America. For Shirley, he is a symbol of opportunity in America.
OTHER BOOKS: *Spring Moon*

CHILD OF THE OWL
Laurence Yep
Dell Publishing Co., 1978
Tough, street-wise Casey is taken to live with her grandmother Paw-

Paw in a run-down flat in Chinatown, where she discovers her people and heritage.
OTHER BOOKS: *Dragonwings; The Serpent's Children; Dragon of the Lost Sea; Dragon Steel; Sweetwater.*

UNCLAIMED TREASURES
Patricia MacLachlan
Harper Trophy, 1987
Willa's wish is to do something extraordinary, but when she falls in love, it isn't at all the way she dreamed it would be.
OTHER BOOKS: *Sarah, Plain and Tall; Arthur for the Very First Time; Cassie Binegar; Seven Kisses in a Row.*

A TASTE OF BLACKBERRIES
Doris Buchanan Smith
Scholastic, 1973
Jamie is a tease and a joker. Then tragedy strikes when Jamie is struck by a swarm of bees.
OTHER BOOKS: *Last Was Lloyd; The First Hard Times; Return to Bitter Creek.*

THE SUMMER OF THE SWANS
Betsy Byars
Avon Camelot, 1974
Sara's mentally retarded younger brother loves to watch the summer swans. When Charlie disappears, Sara realizes what it means to love someone more than yourself. Winner of the Newbery Medal.
OTHER BOOKS: *Cracker Jackson*

THE WOODEN PEOPLE
Myra Paperny
Overlea House, 1987
This is a story of the clash of values in an immigrant family in the late 1920's. Winner of the Canada Council Award for Juvenile Literature.
OTHER BOOKS: *Take a Giant Step*

THE SIGN OF THE BEAVER
Elizabeth George Speare
Dell Yearling, 1984
Until the day his father returns to their cabin in the Maine wilderness, twelve-year-old Matt must try to survive on his own. He is attacked by swarming bees, and rescued by an Indian chief and his grandson, Attean. A Newbery Honor Book.
OTHER BOOKS: *The Witch of Blackbird Pond; The Bronze Bow.*

NOBODY'S FAMILY IS GOING TO CHANGE
Louise Fitzhugh
Dell Yearling, 1975
Emma Sheridan has two concerns in life: eating and becoming a lawyer as soon as possible. Even though Mr. Sheridan is a lawyer himself, he can't imagine his daughter—a female—addressing a courtroom. Emma's little brother, Willie, has one overriding dream—to be a dancer like his Uncle Dipsey. Willie's parents don't think dancing is what their son should be doing.

JOURNEY TO AMERICA
Sonia Levitin
Aladdin, 1987
In 1938, German Jews were faced with more and more restrictions. Lisa Platt was scared of the Nazi Power. Her father plans to escape and leave for America where he hopes to find a better life for Lisa, her mother, and her two sisters.
OTHER BOOKS: *The Return; The Mark of Conte.*

ON MY HONOR
Marion Dane Bauer
Clarion Books, 1986
Joel comes to understand the power of choice after his daredevil friend drowns in a raging river. A Newbery Honor Book.
OTHER BOOKS: *Rain of Fire; Foster Child; Tangled Butterfly; Shelter from the Wind.*

Themes: Sports

S.O.R. LOSERS
Avi
Bradbury Press, 1984
The South Orange River (S.O.R.) Losers are the winningest team in town despite their humiliating performances on the soccer field.

RABBIT EARS
Alfred Slote
J.B. Lippincott, 1982
Tip was a great pitcher in the younger league, but now that he's moved up, he can't seem to take the jeering from opposing teams. Since he developed rabbit ears, he can't even get the ball over the plate.
OTHER BOOKS: *Tony and Me; My Father, the Coach; Hang Tough, Paul Mather; The Biggest Victory; Stranger on the Ball Club.*

MINI-BIKE RACER
Claire Mackay
Scholastic-TAB, 1976
In this sequel to *Mini-Bike Hero*, Kim Chambers joins forces with Julie and Jake to pull off a daring rescue, only to learn that some things are more important than winning.
SERIES: *Mini-Bike Hero; Mini-Bike Rescue.*

THE YEAR MOM WON THE PENNANT
Matt Christopher
Little, Brown & Company, 1968
The Thunderballs are winners for the first time in their history, and it's Nick's Mom who coaches them through the mad race for the Pennant.

HOCKEYBAT HARRIS
Geoffrey Bilson
Kids Can Press, 1984
David arrives in Canada from Britian in 1940 and must adjust to his new culture and new way of playing the game.

MARGARET IN THE MIDDLE
Bernice Thurman Hunter
Scholastic-TAB, 1986
This story picks up where *A Place for Margaret* left off. Margaret has settled into her new life on her aunt and uncle's farm when her sister comes to visit and upsets Margaret's delicate balance.
SERIES: *A Place for Margaret*

KING OF THE WIND
Marguerite Henry
Rand McNally, 1948
The history of the great Godolphin Arabian that changed the physical conformation of race horses.
OTHER BOOKS: *Justin Morgan Had a Horse; One Man's Horse; Misty of Chincoteague; Stormy, Misty's Foal; Mustang, Wild Spirit of the West.*

THE BLACK STALLION RETURNS
Walter Farley
Random House, 1944
An Arab chieftain who appeared with ownership papers for Alec's beloved horse takes the Black Stallion to its desert birthplace. This sequel to *The Black Stallion* tells the story of Alec's quest for his stallion—all the way across the Great Desert of Arabia.

SERIES: *The Black Stallion; The Black Stallion's Filly; The Son of the Black Stallion; The Blood Bay Colt.*

ABOUT THE B'NAI BAGELS
E.L. Konigsburg
Atheneum, 1969
Mark's mother becomes manager of his little league baseball team, and his brother joins the team as coach, much to Mark's dismay.

THE KID FROM TOMKINSVILLE
John R. Tunis
Harcourt Brace Jovanovich, 1940
Tunis's characters are men who strive to succeed in a demanding game and who win because of perseverance and talent. These stories reveal some of the problems and prejudices that plagued professional baseball in the past.
OTHER BOOKS: *World Series; Keystone Kids; Rookie of the Year.*

Themes: Biography

KAREN KAIN: BORN TO DANCE
Meguido Zola
Grolier, 1983
This book includes events in the life of this Canadian prima ballerina, and a realistic portrayal of what it is like to be a ballerina —the sacifices, the joys, the setbacks, and the triumphs.
OTHER BOOKS: *Gretzky! Gretzky! Gretzky!; Terry Fox.*

THE WRIGHT BROTHERS AT KITTY HAWK
Donald J. Sobol
Scholastic, 1961
The odds are against them, but in 1903 two bicycle salesmen were able to do what no man had yet done and fly a powered machine. This is the story of their attempts to build the machine themselves and to pursue man's dream to fly.

AMERICAN TALL TALES
Adrien Stoutenberg
Penguin, 1966
These are the stories of eight brave men, such as Paul Bunyan, Pecos Bill, Davy Crockett, Johnny Appleseed, and John Henry.

LAURA INGALLS WILDER
Patricial Reilly Giff
Viking Kestrel, 1987
Laura Ingalls Wilder was a pioneer girl, traveling with her family across unsettled territory, facing times of illness and hardship, yet always loving the great open prairie. Years later, Laura wanted to record the events of her childhood for her own daughter, Rose. These stories became the greatly loved *Little House* books.
OTHER BOOKS: *Mother Theresa*

CHILD OF THE SILENT NIGHT
Edith Fisher Hunter
Dell Publishing Co., 1971
This is a biography of a young girl, Laura Bridgman, coping with her disabilities in the early nineteenth century. Like Helen Keller, she suffered from an illness that left her both blind and deaf.

MARK'S WHEELCHAIR ADVENTURES
Camilla Jessel
Methuen, 1987
This is the story of a boy with spina bifida who copes with the discomfort of moving, of making friends, and of moving around, in a wheelchair.

MARCHING TO FREEDOM: THE STORY OF MARTIN LUTHER KING, JR.
Joyce Milton
Parachute Press, 1987
A biography of Martin Luther King, Jr., the charismatic black leader and his movement for civil rights freedom.

FREEDOM TRAIN: THE STORY OF HARRIET TUBMAN
Dorothy Sterling
Scholastic, 1954
Harriet Tubman escaped to the north by the secret route called the "Underground Railroad" and led over 300 black people on a dangerous route to freedom. This is the story of her bold and courageous life.

KIPLING
Gloria Kamen
Collier Macmillan, 1985
Kamen presents a brief biography of the teller of tales of the East and West. Kipling's early life in India and England is outlined,

highlighting his later success as reporter, poet, and short story writer.

THE ADVENTURES OF CHARLES DARWIN
Peter Ward
Cambridge, 1986
George Carter, cabin boy, spends five years sailing the seas and sharing exciting adventures with Charles Darwin, the ship's naturalist. They ride with the gauchos in Argentina and unravel some of the secrets of the Galapagos Islands with their great tortoises and huge sea dragons.

Themes: Fantasy

THE IRON MAN
Ted Hughes
Faber Paperbacks, 1968
The coming of the iron man signals an adventure in fantasy until the very end when the iron man and the space-bat-angel-dragon battle for power.

MY TRIP TO ALPHA 1
Alfred Slote
Avon Camelot, 1980
Traveling between planets by Voya-Code is the best way to travel, and Jack is the first member of his family to try it.

HALF MAGIC
Edward Eager
Harcourt Brace Jovanovich, 1970
An ordinary summer becomes an extraordinary adventure when four young children, who have been reading the magic books of E. Nesbit, stumble on a magical world of their own.
OTHER BOOKS: *Knight's Castle; Magic by the Lake; The Time Garden.*

THE WISH GIVER: THREE TALES OF COVEN TREE
Bill Brittain
Harper Trophy, 1986
The sign outside a shabby old tent at the annual Tree Church Social reads:

THADDEUS BLINN
I CAN GIVE YOU
WHATEVER YOU ASK FOR
ONLY 50¢

Only four people are curious and venture to discover that wishes come true. A Newbery Honor Book.
OTHER BOOKS: *All the Money in the World; Devil's Donkey.*

THE WHITE STAG
Kate Seredy
Penguin, 1979
This heroic legend is the epic story of a tribe's migration from Asia to Europe, led by their fierce leader Attilla. Winner of the Newbery Award.
OTHER BOOKS: *The Good Master*

TUCK EVERLASTING
Natalie Babbitt
Bantam Skylark, 1976
The story of a family named Tuck who find a small clearing, and in it the hidden source of life everlasting.
OTHER BOOKS: *Goody Hall; The Search for Delicious; Knee-Knock Rise; The Eye of the Amaryllis.*

THE ENCHANTED CASTLE
E. Nesbit
Buccaneer Books, 1981
Gerald, Cathy, and Jimmy discover an enchanted garden. There they wake a beautiful princess from a hundred-year sleep, only to have her immediately made invisible by a magic ring.
OTHER BOOKS: *The Railway Children; (Trilogy); The Story of the Treasure-Seekers; The New Treasure-Seekers; The Wouldbegoods.*

THE KELPIE'S PEARLS
Mollie Hunter
Harper & Row Publishers, 1976
Some people didn't believe in the Loch Ness Monster, but Torquil believed in the kelpie that raised it too, for he'd seen the water-spirit talking to Morag.
OTHER BOOKS: *The Wicked One; A Stranger Came Ashore; The Walking Stones; The Smartest Man in Ireland.*

THE BOOK OF THREE
Lloyd Alexander
Dell Publishing Co., 1964
The land of Prydain is threatened by the evil forces of King Arawan, the Death-Lord. Taran, the Assistant Pig-Keeper, is the unlikely leader of the struggle against the forces of evil. This tale of

enchantment runs through five novels that can be read separately or as a series.

SERIES: *Chronicles of Prydain: The Book of Three; The Black Cauldron; The Castle of Llyr; Taran Wanderer; The High King.*

OTHER BOOKS: *The Foundling and Other Tales of Prydain; The Cat Who Wished to Be a Man; The Wizard in the Tree; The El Dorado Adventure.*

Themes: Historical Fiction

SADAKO AND THE THOUSAND PAPER CRANES
Eleanor Coerr
Dell Yearling, 1979
When the atom bomb was dropped, the families who lived in Hiroshima faced the ever-present danger of a disease. Young Sadako contacts leukemia and is told by her friend Chizuko that if she folds a thousand paper cranes God will make her well again.

THE STAINED GLASS WINDOW
Penelope Lively
Abelard-Schuman, 1980
A knight and a lady are depicted upon the stained glass window. A girl named Jane began to wonder who they were and why a window was made in their memory, and we begin to learn the story of a knight leaving his lady for a crusade.

THE HOUSE OF SIXTY FATHERS
Meindert De Jong
Harper & Row Publishers, 1956
A World War II story about a Chinese boy and his pet pig who make a desperate journey to find the boy's family.

THE HAND OF ROBIN SQUIRES
Joan Clark
Penguin, 1977
An eighteenth-century English boy is brought to Oak Island, off Nova Scotia, by his pirate uncle. The boy is forced to work with black slaves to dig the shafts where treasure is to be buried, and escapes only with the help of a Micmac friend.

WHITE MIST
Barbara Smucker
Irwin Publishing, 1985
May Appleby and Lee Pokagon suddenly find themselves in the

thriving nineteenth-century logging town of Singapore. Summoned back in time by a mysterious Indian chief, the two teenagers react differently to their startling adventure.

OTHER BOOKS: *Days of Terror; Amish Adventure; Underground to Canada.*

JUMP SHIP TO FREEDOM
James Lincoln Collier & Christopher Collier
Dell Yearling, 1981
Young Daniel Arabus and his mother are slaves. By law they should be free, since Daniel's father fought in the Revolutionary Army and earned enough in soldiers' notes to buy his family's freedom. When Daniel's caught stealing, he is forced aboard a ship bound for the West Indies—and certain slavery.

SEQUELS: *War Comes to Willy Freeman; Who is Carrie?*

CHARLEY SKEDADDLE
Patricia Beatty
William Morrow & Company, 1987
A story of a young boy's journey to manhood as he flees both from the Union Army he has deserted and from the Confederates who would arrest him as a spy.

OTHER BOOKS: *Behave Yourself, Bethany Bryant; Turn Homeward, Hannalee; Eight Mules from Monterey; Melinda Takes a Hand; The Coach That Never Came; Red Rock over the River; Wait For me, Watch For Me, Eula Bee; Jonathan Down Under.*

THE DOOR IN THE WALL
Marguerite de Angeli
Doubleday, 1949
Brother Luke takes Robin to a monastery where he will be cared for until his father sends for him. When the message comes at last, Robin makes a dangerous journey to a castle which is under attack. Winner of the Newbery Medal.

OTHER BOOKS: *Thee, Hannah!*

Themes: Nature

THE TROUBLE WITH TUCK
Theodore Taylor
Avon Camelot, 1983
Helen loves her dog Tuck, so when he begins to lose his sight, Helen fights to be his eyes.

OTHER BOOKS: *The Cay; The Odyssey of Ben O'Neal.*

THE MIDNIGHT FOX
Betsy Byars
Puffin, 1981
Tom was being forced to live on a farm. This holds countless terrors for him until he meets the midnight fox.
OTHER BOOKS: *The House of Wings; The Summer of the Swans.*

OWLS IN THE FAMILY
Farley Mowat
Atlantic Little, Brown, 1961
There were already gophers, rats, snakes, pigeons, and a dog in the family, so an owl didn't seem so overwhelming. Billy is faced with keeping animals and humans separate and happy.
OTHER BOOKS: *Lost in the Barrens; The Dog Who Wouldn't Be.*

THE BATTLE OF BUBBLE AND SQUEAK
Philippa Pearce
Puffin, 1980
Even though Sidana, Peggy, and Amy adore the two gerbils, their mother detests them. A family battle occurs.
OTHER BOOKS: *Tom's Midnight Garden*

CALL IT COURAGE
Armstrong Sperry
Macmillan, 1971
Mafatu's name means Stout Heart, but he fears the sea because it killed his mother when he was a baby. One day, alone in his canoe, he paddles out to sea to conquer his fear. A Newbery Award winner.

SOUNDER
William Armstrong
Harper & Row Publishers, 1972
When his father is arrested and Sounder the family dog is shot and wounded, Sam learns about inhuman oppression, and the strength of family life.

WHERE THE RED FERN GROWS
Wilson Rawls
Bantam Books, 1974
Old Dan had the brawn, Little Ann had the brains—and Billy had the will to train them to be the finest hunting team in the valley.

Themes: Humor

BUNNICULA
Deborah and James Howe
Avon Camelot, 1980
Chester, a very well-read cat, and Harold the dog knew there was something strange about the bunny who seemed to have fangs. When the vegetables were drained white and dry, the two characters were sure that Bunnicula was indeed a vampire rabbit.
SEQUELS: *The Celery Stalks at Midnight; Howliday Inn; Nighty Nightmare.*
OTHER BOOKS: *Morgan's Zoo*

CHOCOLATE FEVER
Robert Kimmel Smith
Dell Yearling, 1972
Harry Green loved chocolate—any kind, served in any way—more than any boy in the world's history. One day, however, Henry breaks medical history by breaking out in brown bumps with the world's first case of chocolate fever.
OTHER BOOKS: *Jelly Belly; Mostly Michael; The War with Grandpa.*

SOUP
Robert Newton Peck
Dell Publishing Co., 1974
The comic stories and troubles of a special friendship between Rob and Soup, from a boyhood filled with barrels to roll in, apples to whip, windows to break, ropes to bind prisoners, acorn pipes, and ten-cent Saturday movies.
SEQUELS: *Soup and Me; Soup on Wheels; Soup for President; Soup on Ice.*
OTHER BOOKS: *Trig; Trig Sees Red; Trig or Treat; Mr. Little; Banjo.*

ARABEL AND MORTIMER
Joan Aiken
Dell Yearling, 1983
Mortimer the ever-hungry raven floats out to sea to get even with the giraffes who stole his doughnuts at the zoo.
SEQUELS: *Arabel's Raven; Mortimer Says Nothing.*

THE SHEEP PIG
Dick King-Smith; ill. Mary Rayner
Victor Gollancz, 1983
Fly, the sheep-dog, teaches Babe, the pig, all there is to know about herding sheep. Winner of the Guardian Children's Fiction Award.

OTHER BOOKS: *Daggie Dogfoot; The Fox Busters; Harry's Mad; Magnus Powermouse; The Mouse Butcher; Pets for Keeps; The Queen's Nose.*

THE PIEMAKERS
Helen Cresswell
J.B. Lippincott, 1968
Being piemakers was a serious business to the Danby Rollers. Their own secret and their shameful failure made success in the King's great piemaking contest more important than ever.
OTHER BOOKS: *Bagthorpes; Bagthorpes Abroad; Bagthorpes Haunted; Bagthorpes Unlimited; Bagthorpes V.S. the World; Ordinary Jack; Absolute Zero; The Secret World of Polly Flint; Lizzie Dripping.*

THE BEST CHRISTMAS PAGEANT EVER
Barbara Robinson
Avon Camelot, 1979
The worst kids in the history of the world become part of the annual Christmas pageant.

THE GREAT SMILE ROBBERY
Roger McGough
Puffin, 1984
Emerson has a cupboard full of smiles—warm-hearted ones, cheeky ones, shy ones, sad ones, and just a few he's made up himself. He should be able to easily win the nationwide smiling competition but the Stinker Gang have other plans.

THE WAR AT FORT MAGGIE
Raymond Bradbury
Kids Can Press, 1981
An account of the adventures of a class outing to historic Fort Maggie. The story is presented through journal entries and tape transcripts.

THE GREAT BRAIN
John D. Fitzgerald
Dell Publishing Co., 1967
The first title in the popular series about Tom O. Fitzgerald a.k.a. the Great Brain. The stories about this scheming 10-year-old are told from the point of view of his admiring younger brother.
SERIES: *More Adventures of the Great Brain; The Great Brain Reforms; The Return of the Great Brain; The Great Brain at the Academy; Me and My Little Brain; The Great Brain does it Again.*

Popular Books

Over the years, such books as the Hardy Boys and Nancy Drew have remained popular with children in the middle years. The children enjoy the familiar plot structures and take comfort in the stock heroes that accompany the narrative. Peer groups have their own power in determining what children want to read, and adults must recognize this if they hope to influence the reading materials selected by this group. By providing similar books in theme, yet stronger in artistic merit, adults can bring the young reader gently to an awareness of other appropriate novels, and begin building the literary foundation of future readers.

ENCYCLOPEDIA BROWN, BOY DETECTIVE
Donald J. Sobol
Bantam Skylark, 1963
Readers are invited to weigh the facts and solve the mystery in ten cases.
OTHER BOOKS: *There are two dozen titles in this series, such as: Encyclopedia Brown Finds the Clues; Encyclopedia Brown Gets His Man.*

MURDER ON THE CANADIAN
Eric Wilson
Totem, 1982
This is a Tom Austen Mystery where the hero investigates a murder plot aboard a sleek passenger train.
OTHER BOOKS: *Vancouver Nightmare; The Ghost of Lunenberg Manor; Terror in Winnipeg; The Lost Treasure of Casa Loma; Disneyland Hostage.*

THE SECRET OF THE SUN GOD
Andrea Packard
Bantam Books, 1987
There are over 65 titles in these popular Choose Your Own Adventure stories where the reader decides how the story will end. In "The Secret of the Sun God" the reader is flown to Mexico to discover an ancient lost civilization.
SERIES: *The Mummy's Tomb; Jungle Safari; Help! You're Shrinking; India Trail; Trouble in Space.*

THIS CAN'T BE HAPPENING AT MACDONALD HALL
Gordon Korman
Scholastic-TAB, 1978
Bruno and Boots are at the bottom of the chaos at Macdonald Hall.

When the headmaster decides to separate the two boys, he thinks his troubles are over, but they're just beginning.
OTHER BOOKS: *Beware the Fish; Bruno and Boots; Our Man Weston; No Coins, Please; Go Jump in the Pool!; The War With Mr. Wizzle.*

SUPERFUDGE
Judy Blume
Dell Publishing Co., 1981
This sequel to *Tales of a Fourth Grade Nothing* continues the experiences of Peter Hatcher. With his younger brother in the first grade in the same school as Peter and another baby on the way, Peter thinks the only solution is to pack his bag and leave home.
OTHER BOOKS: *Tales of a Fourth Grade Nothing; Are You There God? It's Me, Margaret; The One in the Middle is a Green Kangaroo; Freckle Juice; Blubber; Otherwise Known as Sheila the Great; Then Again, Maybe I Won't.*

A LIGHT IN THE ATTIC
Shel Silverstein
Harper & Row Publishers, 1981
In the attic of Shel Silverstein you will find Backward Bill, Sour Face Ann, the Meehoo with an Exactlywatt, and the Polar Bear in the Frigidaire, in a collection of poems and drawings.
OTHER BOOKS: *Where the Sidewalk Ends; The Giving Tree.*

Classics

For generations, children in the middle years have enjoyed a body of novels that seem never to age or date. Because of the universal truths that hold constant, children can read or listen to books that portray a different life from their own in custom, place, time, or circumstance. For some children, these differences make the reading difficult, and the stories may have to be read to them. However, independent readers may relish the depth of language and content that make up classics.

CHARLOTTE'S WEB
E.B. White; ill. Garth Williams
Scholastic, 1952
Wilbur the barn pig is bored and lonely until he meets Charlotte the spider who thinks of a plan to save Wilbur from an unhappy fate.
OTHER BOOKS: *Stuart Little; The Trumpet of the Swan.*

HOMER PRICE
Robert McCloskey
Puffin, 1976
Six epidosdes in the life of Homer Price, including one in which he
and his pet skunk capture four bandits and another about a donut
machine on the rampage.
SEQUEL: *Centerburg Tales*

THE WIZARD OF OZ
L. Frank Baum
1900; many editions
Dorothy Gale is whisked from Kansas to the magical land of Oz
where—with a Scarecrow, a Tin Woodman, and a Cowardly Lion—
she sets off to find the illusive Wizard.
SERIES: *Dorothy and the Wizard of Oz; The Patchwork Girl of Oz; The
Land of Oz; Ozma of Oz; The Road to Oz; The Emerald City of Oz; The
Scarecrow of Oz; Rinkitink of Oz; The Lost Princess of Oz; The Tin
Woodman of Oz; The Magic of Oz; Glinda of Oz.*

ANNE OF GREEN GABLES
L.M. Montgomery
1908; Putnam Publishing Group, 1983
The story of a young orphan girl living in Prince Edward island.
SERIES: *Anne of the Island; Anne of the Windy Poplars; Anne's House of
Dreams; Anne of Ingleside; Rainbow Valley; Rilla of Ingleside; Chronicles of
Avonlea; Further Chronicles of Avonlea.*

LITTLE HOUSE IN THE BIG WOODS
Laura Ingalls Wilder
1932; Harper & Row Publishers, 1953
These 19th century frontier stories describe the growing up of the
Ingalls girls and the Wilder boys.
SERIES: *Little House on the Prairie; Farmer Boy; Little Town on the Prairie;
On the Banks of Plum Creek; These Happy Golden Years.*

THE BORROWERS
Mary Norton; ill. Beth and Joe Krush
Harcourt Brace Jovanovich, 1965
The Borrowers are tiny people who live out of sight in old houses,
subsisting on what they can "borrow" from "human beans."
Homily, Pod, and their daughter Arriety were surprised to find a

Boy in the old house when none had been around for years.
SERIES: *The Borrowers Aloft; The Borrowers Afield; The Borrowers Afloat; The Borrowers Avenged.*

THE SECRET GARDEN
Frances Hodgson Burnett
1909; Dell Publishing Co., 1962
Mary, an orphan, discovers a locked garden on her Uncle's Yorkshire Estate. She becomes friends with Dickon and Colin, and overcomes emotional and physical difficulties.
OTHER BOOKS: *A Little Princess; Little Lord Fauntleroy.*

Information Books

Children today have access to a wide variety of informative, non-fiction books which cover almost every interest they may have as well as many aspects of the school curriculum. Authors, essayists, artists, and photographers are producing excellent books that not only inform but present points of view, personal statements, attitudes, and feelings. While some books may fill the interest needs of the child, the writing itself may prove difficult. However, captions, photographs, charts and brief annotations may be within the readability level of the child. In small groups or with an enabling adult, children can satisfy their curiosity and questions with high quality information books. The selections in the following list are only representative of the materials available for children today.

THE GIANT BOOK OF STRANGE BUT TRUE SPORTS STORIES
Howard Liss; ill. Joe Mathier
Random House, 1976
This reference book will delight sports enthusiasts as well as those readers who enjoy reading fascinating information.

GIANTS OF LAND, SEA & AIR
David Peters
Alfred A. Knopf, 1986
Seventy-one of the largest animals of all time are compared to humans and to each other, in full-color paintings, all drawn to the same scale. Fold-out sections open to show the biggest of the big. A capsule biography of each giant describes its life on earth.

THE GREAT WALL OF CHINA
Leonard Everett Fisher
Macmillan, 1986
Facts concerning the Great Wall are reported in straightforward narration, such as how many workers built the wall, how long it took, and how big it was, along with illustrations that add to the power of the information.

A KID'S FIRST BOOK ABOUT SEX
Joani Blank; ill. Marcia Quackenbush
Down There Press, 1982
Blank addresses body image, masturbation, touching, and sexual partnerships. She assumes that the book is being shared by adult and child and directs questions to the adult.

READING, WRITING AND RUMMY
Margie Golick, Ph.D.
Pembroke Publishers, 1986
More than 100 card games to develop language, social skills, number concepts, and problem-solving strategies.

SCIENCEWORKS
Ontario Science Centre; ill. Tina Holdcroft
Kids Can Press, 1984
Six major categories of experiments from *The Great Outdoors* to *things to make* provide teachers and students with real "hands-on" science.
OTHER BOOKS: *Foodworks*

THE SUN
Seymour Simon
William Morrow & Company, 1986
In over twenty full-colour photographs and a clear, informative text, Simon describes the sun, from the constant nuclear explosions to the boiling gases that form the surface.
OTHER BOOKS: *Icebergs and Glaciers*

SUPER STRING GAMES
Camilla Gryski; ill. Tom Sankey
Kids Can Press, 1987
The newest collection of more than twenty unusual and amazing string figures. Each of the figures comes with easy-to-follow, step-by-step instructions.
OTHER BOOKS: *Cat's Cradle, Owl's Eyes; Many Stars and More String Games.*

VOLCANO
Patricia Lauber
Bradbury Press, 1986
This book describes the eruption and healing of Mount St. Helens. A Newbery Honor Book.
OTHER BOOKS: *Journey to the Planets*

Read Aloud/Tell Aloud

Sometimes adults forget that children in the middle years are especially needful of hearing stories read aloud. Through modelling, the adult demonstrates the importance of reading, their attitude toward print, and the satisfaction of a story. They can share literary selections, styles, and vocabulary that may be absorbed by the child. By choosing books that children themselves may not, or by selecting stories from other countries and cultures, the adult brings a sophisticated, multi-levelled approach to the processes of finding out and investigating. Children need to apply their gains from novel reading to the world of information.

ABEL'S ISLAND
William Steig
Bantam Skylark, 1977
The tale of a lovable mouse isolated on a beautiful island, told in Victorian style.
OTHER BOOKS: *Dominic*

ALL THE KING'S HORSES
Michael Foreman
Hamish Hamilton, 1976
The story of a princess who "wasn't the milk-white, golden-haired pink little number the way princesses are supposed to be." A satirical folk tale using traditional forms to demonstrate female independence.
OTHER BOOKS: *War and Peas; Panda and the Bushfire.*

THE CRANE WIFE
retold by Sumiko Yagawa; translation from the Japanese by Katherine Paterson; ill. Suekichi Akaba
Mulberry, 1987
Soon after he rescues a wounded crane from death a poor farmer is visited by a lovely stranger who asks to become his wife. She is a mysterious woman who weaves cloth of unearthly brilliance.

DAWN
Molly Bang
William Morrow & Company, 1983
A moving tale of a poor shipbuilder who rescues a wounded Canada goose, releases it, and soon meets a mysterious and beautiful woman who weaves sails known as the Wings of Steel.
OTHER BOOKS: *The Paper Crane; The Grey Lady and the Strawberry Snatcher; Wiley and the Hairy Man.*

THE HOBBIT
J.R.R. Tolkien
George Allen & Unwin, 1937
Encounters with trolls, goblins, dwarves, elves, and giant spiders are some of the adventures that befall Bilbo Baggins.
SEQUEL: *The Lord of the Rings*

LOST AND FOUND
Jill Paton Walsh; ill. Mary Rayner
Andre Deutsch, 1985
Beginning with an arrowhead in prehistoric days and ending with a pair of scissors in modern times, this story traces a series of items lost and found through the passage of time.
OTHER BOOKS: *Babylon*

THE MAGICIAN'S NEPHEW
C.S. Lewis
Fontana Lions, 1980
There are seven stories about the mythical land of Narnia, and this book explains how all the adventures began.
SERIES: *The Chronicles of Narnia: The Lion, the Witch and the Wardrobe; Prince Caspian; The Voyage of the Dawn Treader; The Silver Chair; The Horse and His Boy; The Last Battle.*

THE MOUSE AND HIS CHILD
Russell Hoban; ill. Lillian Hoban
Avon Camelot, 1974
The story of a tin father and son who dance under a Christmas tree until they break the ancient clockwork rules and are themselves broken. Thrown away and then rescued by a tramp, they set out on a dangerous odyssey to follow a dream of finding a home.
OTHER BOOKS: *The Flight of Bembel Rudzuk*

SARAH, PLAIN AND TALL
Patricia MacLachlan
Harper & Row Publishers, 1985
Papa places an ad in the newspaper for a wife and he receives an answer from a woman named Sarah, who lives in Maine. Sarah writes, "I will come by train. I will wear a yellow bonnet. I am plain and tall." Winner of the Newbery Award.
OTHER BOOKS: *Cassie Binegar; Arthur for the Very First Time; Unclaimed Treasures; Through Grandpa's Eyes.*

STIG OF THE DUMP
Clive King
Puffin, 1963
Barney is wandering on the edge of an abandoned chalk-pit when he falls into a sort of cave. He meets Stig, who has a lot of shaggy hair, wears a rabbit-skin, and speaks in grunts.
OTHER BOOKS: *Ninny's Boat; Me and My Million; The Seashore People.*

THE STONE BOOK QUARTET
Alan Garner
William Collins Sons, 1978
The history of a Cheshire village family of craftspeople from the 1860's to World War II is traced in this quartet of books, based on Garner's family history. Each story is interwoven with the others.

STONE FOX
John Reynolds Gardiner; ill. Marcia Sewall
Harper Trophy, 1980
The story of the race between a boy, his sled dog, and the Indian, Stone Fox.

WHEN I WAS YOUNG IN THE MOUNTAINS
Cynthia Rylant; ill. Diane Goode
E.P. Dutton Books, 1982
A warm reminiscence of a childhood spent in the Appalachian mountains with loving grandparents.
OTHER BOOKS: *A Blue-Eyed Daisy; A Fine White Dust.*

THE WIND IN THE WILLOWS
Kenneth Grahame
1908; many editions
This book evokes the beauty of the natural world, the love of one's own home-place, and the charm of small wild creatures.

Picture Books for Sharing

Like some films, a picture book can be a pleasure for an audience spanning a wide age range. Just as Mary Poppins, Swiss Family Robinson, and Star Wars can be viewed by the whole family, children in the middle years can share in the delight of the picture book. This medium allows them to experience stories, memoirs, concepts, and dreams as interpreted by authors and artists using photography, collage, parity, etches, and oils. The text within a picture book must be written concisely and with the art in mind, so children gain a particular and effective communication package. Since picture books were designed to be read aloud, the children can experience the literature through the ear and the eye, and perhaps be touched by the emotional quality inherent in this art form.

DAKOTA DUGOUT
Ann Turner; ill. Ronald Himler
Macmillan, 1985
A granddaughter is told what it was like to live in a sod house on the Dakota prairie a century ago. The poetic text and sensitive drawings describe life on the prairie as the pioneers knew it.
OTHER BOOKS: *Nettie's Trip South*

DEATH OF THE IRON HORSE
Paul Goble
Bradbury Press, 1987
An Indian attack in 1867 on a freight train is told from the Indians' point-of-view.
OTHER BOOKS: *Buffalo Woman; The Girl Who Loved Wild Horses; The Gift of The Sacred Dog.*

EYES OF THE DRAGON
Margaret Leaf; ill. Ed Young
Lothrop, Lee & Shepard, 1987
An artist agrees to paint a dragon on the wall of a Chinese village, but the magistrate's insistence that he paint eyes on the dragon has amazing results.

HARALD AND THE GIANT KNIGHT
Donald Carrick
Clarion Books, 1982
A medieval story about a boy who outwits the thoughtless knights who have turned his family's farm into a jousting arena.

I'M IN CHARGE OF CELEBRATIONS
Byrd Baylor; ill. Peter Parnall
Charles Scribner's Sons, 1986
Baylor draws us into her natural world in her poetic descriptions of
108 private celebrations.
OTHER BOOKS: *The Other Way To Listen; When Clay Sings; The Desert Is
Theirs; The Way To Start the Day; The Best Town in the World; Hawk,
I'm Your Brother; Everybody Needs A Rock; Your Own Best Secret Place.*

THE MIRRORSTONE
Michael Palin; ill. Alan Lee, Richard Seymour
Jonathon Cape, 1986
A unique looking-glass adventure of time, space and imagination,
including seven magical holograms that appear within.

A NORTHERN ALPHABET
Ted Harrison
Tundra Books, 1982
Each letter of the alphabet is accompanied by a painting and a brief
text that names only a few of the objects, animals, and people
illustrated. Each painting is a depiction of life in the North and is
also the beginning of a story which readers are encouraged to finish.
OTHER BOOKS: *Children of the Yukon; The Cremation of Sam McGee.*

THE PAINTER AND THE WILD SWANS
Claude Clément; ill. Frédéric Clément
Dial Books, 1986
This is the story of Teiji, a renowned Japanese painter, who one day
sees a flock of wild swans pass overhead. In that instant he knows
that until he captures the beauty of the birds on canvas, he will not
paint again.

THE RAINBOW GOBLINS
Ul de Rico
Warner Books, 1978
The dramatic illustrations tell the story of the valley which goblins
have invaded to capture and swallow the rainbow.

ROUND TRIP
Ann Jonas
Greenwillow Books, 1983
The reader travels through the story from beginning to end and then
turns around to come back. This simple trick is displayed in black
and white drawings.

SAILING WITH THE WIND
Thomas Locker
Dial Books, 1986
A young girl discovers the ocean's majestic character when she joins her uncle on a sailing trip. This journey not only gives Elizabeth a taste of the world but of herself as well.
OTHER BOOKS: *Where The River Begins; The Mare On The Hill; The Ugly Duckling.*

THE SORCERER'S APPRENTICE
Robin Muller
Kids Can Press, 1985
This familiar tale of a boy who wants to become a sorcerer is accompanied by detailed illustrations that complement the fantasy aspect of the story.
OTHER BOOKS: *Tatterhood*

THE STRANGER
Chris Van Allsburg
Houghton Mifflin, 1986
A mysterious stranger passes through town and it seems that fall will never come again.
OTHER BOOKS: *The Mysteries of Harris Burdick; The Garden of Abdul Gasazi; Jumanji; The Polar Express; Ben's Dream; The Wreck of the Zephyr.*

Collections

For some children, the short story is a satisfying read, just long enough to be intellectually and emotionally satisfying, yet within the range of concentration and readability. A collection of short stories can present the young reader with suitable material for encouraging him or her to continue reading. Collections can include stories by a single author, stories by several authors arranged by theme or topic, or stories representing the work of a group of authors through various literary forms—poetry, stories, essays—linked together thematically. These anthologies can encourage readers to locate and read other stories, poems, or novels by the same author. They also present children with a variety of viewpoints and styles within the pages of a single text.

FABLES
Arnold Lobel
Harper & Row Publishers, 1980
Twenty original fables, each with a fresh moral, accompanied by beautiful illustrations by the author.

FAIRY TALES
Terry Jones; ill. Michael Foreman
Puffin, 1983
A collection of thirty stories of fantasy and morality which introduces the reader to a rainbow cat, a fly-by-night creature, a corn dolly, and other such magical beings.

HOW THE WHALE BECAME AND OTHER STORIES
Ted Hughes; ill. George Adamson
Penguin, 1971
Long ago when the world was brand new, creatures began to appear from every side, from under leaves, and from behind racks. These stories explain their existence.

THE GIRL WHO CRIED FLOWERS
Jane Yolen; ill. David Palladini
Thomas Y. Crowell, 1974
Five tales of haunting strangeness and adventure. The title story tells of the beautiful Olivia, whose sorrow brought happiness to others as her tears turned magically to flowers.
OTHER BOOKS: *Neptune Rising; Dream Weaver; The Moon Ribbon.*

WHEN SHLEMIEL WENT TO WARSAW AND OTHER STORIES
Isaac Bashevis Singer; ill. Margot Zemach
Farrar, Straus & Giroux, 1968
This collection of eight stories, some inspired by traditional Jewish tales, ranges from comedy to fantasy to parable.
OTHER BOOKS: *Naftali the Storyteller and his Horse, Sus and Other Stories*

THE WINDOW OF DREAMS
edited by Mary Alice Downie, Elizabeth Greene and M.A. Thompson
Methuen, 1986
Almost all of the pieces in this anthology of 30 stories and poems appear in print for the first time. Most are written by well-known Canadian writers.

Traditional Tales

Folktale, "the stories of the tribe," provides strong reading and listening materials for children in the middle years. The context of "long ago" enables the child to explore the universal problems and concerns that have troubled humanity forever, but in a safe, non-threatening framework. The deeds of heroes, the schemes of tricksters, and the lore of nations past can all serve as settings for the child's own development through family situations, societal difficulties, supernatural beliefs, and natural phenomena. The learning and wisdom handed down through folktale can be understood and appreciated by today's children as they experience legends, myths, fairy and folktales retold and illustrated by contemporary authors and artists.

THE VILLAGE OF ROUND AND SQUARE HOUSES
Ann Grifalconi
Little, Brown & Company, 1986
A grandmother explains to her listeners why in their village on the side of a volcano the men live in square houses and the women in round ones.

THE STONE-CUTTER
Gerald McDermott
Puffin, 1978
Tasaku was a lowly stonecutter, but he was very happy in his work until one day a royal prince passed by in a magnificent procession. Then Tasaku wished aloud that he too might have wealth, and the spirit who lives in the mountain heard him.
OTHER BOOKS: *The Magic Tree; Arrow To the Sun; Anansi the Spider; Sunflight.*

THE ENCHANTED CARIBOU
Elizabeth Cleaver
Oxford University Press, 1985
The story of a wandering maiden named Tyya and her rescue by a young caribou hunter, Etosak. Shadow puppets illustrate the episodes of the tale.
OTHER BOOKS: *The Loon's Necklace; The Fire Stealer; The Mountain Goats of Temlaham; How Summer Came To Canada; The Miraculous Hind; Petrouchka.*

THE WEAVING OF A DREAM
Marilee Heyes
Viking Kestrel, 1986
A retelling of a traditional Chinese tale about a beautiful tapestry, woven by a poor woman, which is stolen by fairies. Her three sons set out on a magical journey to retrieve it.

THE SELKIE GIRL
Susan Cooper; ill. Warwick Hutton
A Margaret K. McElderry Book, 1986
Cooper retells this ancient legend from the coasts and islands of Scotland and Ireland about young Donallan and his seal bride—and the fateful ending of their marriage.

THE SEAL MOTHER
Mordicai Gerstein
Dial Books, 1986
A young fismerman spies a seal on a rock. He watches as she sheds her skin and is transformed into a beautiful woman. The fisherman falls in love, hides the seal's skin, and takes her as his wife. The seal's home is the sea, and she cannot be happy forever as a mortal woman.

THE MAGIC ORANGE TREE
Diane Wolkstein
Alfred A. Knopf, 1978
A collection of folktales gathered by the author in Haiti with comments on Haitien folklore.
OTHER BOOKS: *White Wave*

YEH SHEN: A CINDERELLA STORY FROM CHINA
Ai-Ling Louie; edited by Ed Young
Putnam Publishing Group, 1982
This is a Chinese version of the familiar Cinderella story with imaginative watercolor and pastel illustrations.

CANADIAN FAIRY TALES
Eva Martin; ill. Laszlo Gal
Groundwood Books, 1984
A collection of tales from the New World, told in the tradition of Old World storytelling with accompanying illustrations.
OTHER BOOKS: *Tales of the Far North*

TALES FOR THE TELLING
Edna O'Brien; ill. Michael Foreman
Pavilion, 1986
A collection of Irish folk fairy tales which tell of curses, broken promises, fearsome giants, princesses turning into swans, horses that run faster than the wind, and lands whose inhabitants stay forever young.

Poetry

An explosion of poetry for children in the middle years began with the success of Shel Silverstein. The humor, pathos, and wonder that can be created in a few words seem to represent perfectly the needs of these youngsters. The successful poets know both the interests and the nature of children in the middle years; they evoke significant and emotional responses that may surprise adults. Freed from the rhythms and rhymes of the jingles and verses of young children, the writers explore all types of formats of poetry. Children are able to join in the word play because there is intellectual and emotional satisfaction as well.

FIGGIE HOBBIN
Charles Causley; ill. Jill Bennett
Puffin, 1980
As the King in the title poem remarks, "To cure the sickness of the heart, ah—bring me some figgie hobbin!" A collection of very contemporary poems by Causley.

THE FLIGHT OF THE ROLLER COASTER
Raymond Souster
Oberon Press, 1985
Adventures, animals, and sports are represented in this work by one of Canada's most celebrated poets.

FRESH PAINT: NEW POEMS BY EVE MERRIAM
Eve Merriam; ill. David Frampton
Macmillan, 1986
This collection looks at the commonplace with poems that range in tone and content from the serious to the lyrical.
OTHER BOOKS: *Blackberry Ink; Jamboree; A Sky Full of Poems.*

GARGLING WITH JELLY
Brian Patten
Puffin, 1986
Naughty children, cartoon heroes, lonely caretakers, and unhappy ghouls are some subjects of the poems in this collection of verse.
OTHER BOOKS: *Gangsters, Ghosts and Dragonflies*

HAIRY TALES AND NURSERY CRIMES
Michael Rosen; ill. Alan Baker
Fontana Young Lions, 1987
Rosen has changed the structure of familiar nursery tales and rhymes so that youngsters can read about the Wee Bears and Goldisocks or Fried Pepper of Hamelin.
OTHER BOOKS: *Quick Let's Get Out of Here; You Can't Catch Me; Mind Your Own Business; Smelly Jelly Smelly Fish—The Seaside Book.*

HEY WORLD, HERE I AM!
Jean Little; ill. Barbara Di Lella
Kids Can Press, 1986
Kate, a character from Little's early novel "Look Through My Window," holds the centre stage and "writes" the poems in this collection.

I LIKE THIS POEM
edited by Kaye Webb
Puffin, 1979
In celebration of the International Year of the Child, the members of the Puffin Club assembled a unique selection of favorite poems.

THE NEW KID ON THE BLOCK
Jack Prelutsky; ill. James Stevenson
Greenwillow Books, 1984
Prelutsky's poetry presents people and things that children may have never met before.
OTHER BOOKS: *The Headless Horseman Rides Tonight; Nightmares.*

POEMS FOR OVER 10 YEAR OLDS
Kit Wright; ill. Michael Foreman
Puffin, 1984
This anthology collected by the author has poems of ghouls, animals, and nature as well as poems that are simply full of laughter.
OTHER BOOKS: *Poems for 9-Year-Olds and Under*

THE POETRY TROUPE
compiled by Isabel Wilner
The Poetry Troupe, 1977
Over two hundred poems from a variety of children's poets, for
reading aloud by individuals or groups.

THE RANDOM HOUSE BOOK OF POETRY FOR CHILDREN
selected by Jack Prelutsky; ill. Arnold Lobel
Random House, 1983
In this book is a poem for every occasion, and every page is
illustrated by Caldecott Medal winner Arnold Lobel.

SCARY POEMS FOR ROTTEN KIDS
sean o'huigin
Black Moss Press, 1982
The gruesome, the awesome, and the troublesome are included in
this collection by the award-winning poet.
OTHER BOOKS: *The Trouble with Stitches; Well, You Can Imagine; The
Ghost Horse of the Mounties; Atmosfear.*

SPIN A SOFT BLACK SONG
Nikki Giovannie; ill. George Martins
Hill and Wang, 1985
These poems share the common thread of being for and about black
children, with topics such as mommies, haircuts, basketball, and
dreams.

MESSAGES
compiled by Naomi Lewis
Faber & Faber, 1985
A collection that combines the poets of yesterday with contemporary
selections.

MIDNIGHT FOREST
Judith Nicholls
Faber & Faber, 1987
Evocative, mysterious poems blend into an excellent anthology.
OTHER BOOKS: *Magic Mirror*

The Young Adolescent Years

In these beginning years of adolescence, the lives of children are changing drastically. These developments are reflected in both the content of what they read and in their attitudes toward the act of reading. Family patterns are changing. The young people are becoming critical of parents, of adults in authority, and of siblings. They depend more and more on peer groups. Children begin to have models drawn by entertainment stars, by sport heroes, by friends and from books. Future careers are talked about, and they begin to look forward to their own independence, testing their own positions at every stage. Many develop a sense of history and of their own place in society; they are becoming concerned with justice and the unfair treatment of minority groups. They are able to better understand the complexities of issues. Of course, their physical development is a central factor influencing their lives, their relationships, and their identities.

Books may provide insight into these changes, giving young people roles for identification, situations for reflection, and opportunities for examining issues. Authors for this audience tackle complex topics through realistic settings, fantasy, science fiction, and mystery. Poetry gives the young readers sensitive glimpses into all aspects of life and presents intimate pictures for personal experience. Special interest books offer the readers information about hobbies, social problems, world affairs, sports, and heroes. It is also a time for adults to continue to model reading aloud for young people, bringing them stories they might not select, and interpreting the words with power and effect. The brief lists in this section are only representative of the variety of books available to young adolescents. Adults who provide opportunities and materials for them must continue to observe their needs and wants closely.

Fiction for Reluctant and Remedial Readers

The lives of young adolescents are very full of friends, homework, sports, lessons, and chores. At this stage reading may find itself squeezed out of the timetable. However, school success is greatly determined by a child's literacy strengths, so adults must help young people find time for books, give assistance in selecting books, and especially support those readers who as yet are not fluent or independent. It is certainly not too late for these limited readers. Today's authors are providing books for them that are interesting enough to cause the child to continue reading, yet with a reading range that allows success for these young readers. Adults must beware of books labelled "high interest/low vocabulary," since it is most often the search for meaning that drives a reader to continue reading and complete a book. Word-count in a story does not ensure success. Authors who have talent as well as the needs of the young adolescent in mind will create novels that, with continued help from adults, will give children a chance to become literate young people who want to read well.

DON'T CARE HIGH
Gordon Korman
Scholastic-TAB, 1985
The school is called "Don't Care High," a place where the students don't even know the principal's name. Paul Abrams and his new friend Sheldon are determined to alter the apathy of the school.
OTHER BOOKS: *No Coins, Please; Son of Interflux; A Semester in the Life of a Garbage Dump.*

OUTSIDE
Andre Norton
Avon Books, 1975
Sealed into a huge domed city, Kristie and her brother are among the few survivors of a polluted earth. Kristie has seen pictures of grass, trees, and animals of the old earth in the learning centre. When the mysterious Rhyming Man comes by, she follows him to see the Outside.
OTHER BOOKS: *No Night Without Stars; The Zero Stone; Moon of Three Rings; Quag Keep; Spell of the Witch World; Lore of the Witch World; Horn Crown; Garan the Eternal; Merlin's Mirror; Perilous Dreams; Yurth Burden; Star Ka'at; Star Ka'at World.*

FIRST THE GOOD NEWS
Judie Angell
Pacer Books, 1984
Ninth-grader Annabelle Goobitz is after a story for the national
school newspaper contest. She and her friends eventually track
down Hap Rhysbeck, comedian and TV star, but the news they
uncover leaves Annabelle speechless.
OTHER BOOKS: *Secret Selves; Dear Lola; Suds; What's Best For You;
Ronnie and Rosey; In Summertime It's Tuffy; A Word From Our Sponsor.*

TIGER EYES
Judy Blume
Bradbury Press, 1981
Since her father's death, Davey is so afraid she sleeps with a knife
under her pillow. One day Davey meets Wolf, who helps her
discover a world where good adventures welcome those who are free
enough to laugh.
OTHER BOOKS: *It's Not the End of The World; Starring Sally J. Freeman
As Herself; Then Again Maybe I Won't; Deenie; Are You There God, It's
Me Margaret, Just as Long as We're Together.*

TO ALL MY FANS WITH LOVE, FROM SYLVIE
Ellen Conford
Archway, 1983
Sylvie Kraie is a fifteen-year-old girl who decides to leave home to
become a Hollywood star. However, when the money that she has
saved is stolen, Sylvie is forced to make some serious decisions
about her trip and her life.
OTHER BOOKS: *Strictly for Laughs; Felicia the Critic; Dear Lovey Hart, I
Am Desperate; Seven Days to A Brand New Me; Me and The Terrible Two;
If This Is Love, I'll Take Spaghetti; Anything for a Friend; Lenny Kandell,
Smart Aleck.*

WHERE THE LILIES BLOOM
Vera and Bill Cleaver
Signet, 1974
After her father dies, Mary Call, age fourteen, is determined to keep
her Tennessee mountain family together and to prevent her older
sister from marrying a neighbor.
SERIES: *Trial Valley*
OTHER BOOKS: *Grover; Dust of the Earth; I Would Rather Be a Turnip;
Ellen Grae; Lady Ellen Grae; Sugar Blue.*

TEX
S.E. Hinton
Dell Publishing Co., 1979
For fifteen-year-old Tex, life with his older brother Mace would be
fine if only Mace would stop complaining about their father who
stays away too long. The close relationship between the two brothers
is in jeopardy when Mace starts to play the role of the authority
figure.
OTHER BOOKS: *The Outsiders; That Was Then/This Is Now; Rumble Fish.*

DURANGO STREET
Frank Bonham
Dell Publishing Co., 1965
Rufus Henry, on parole, must find a better way to handle problems
than by fighting. This novel about gang wars demonstrates the
problems of a city slum.
OTHER BOOKS: *The Nitty Gritty; Cool Cat; Gimme an H, Gimme an E,
Gimme an L, Gimme a P; The Forever Formula; The Vagabundos;
Premonitions.*

THE PIGMAN
Paul Zindel
Bantam Books, 1981
Mr. Pignate is a lonely old man with an awful secret. John and
Lorraine, two high school sophomores, become his friends. They are
two lonely people who are looking for a way out of their own
loneliness.
SEQUEL: *The Pigman's Legacy*
OTHER BOOKS: *The Undertaker's Gone Bananas; My Darling, My
Hamburger; Pardon Me, You're Stepping on My Eyeball; I Never Loved
Your Mind; Confessions of a Teenage Baboon; The Girl Who Wanted A
Boy; Harry & Hortense at Hormone High.*

Fiction for Developing Readers

Novels for young adolescents allow the reader to engage in a
dialogue with an author on a wide range of topics and at a deep,
emotional level. The personal and private reading of a novel gives
the youngster the security to delve into situations that may touch his
or her life, giving him or her opportunities to identify and reflect
upon human traits and behavior. The themes of these novels reflect
the development of the young adolescents, their concern about their

place in the adult world, ecology, peace, the future, and the past. Adults must understand the need these young readers have for understanding life's problems and accept that the portrayal and examination of these issues, carefully and artfully developed in the novel form, will strengthen the understanding and beliefs of these young people.

BABY SISTER
Marilyn Sachs
E.P. Dutton Books, 1986
Fifteen-year-old Penny adores her stylish older sister, but when her sister goes away to college, Penny must discover her own talents as well as her self.
OTHER BOOKS: *The Fat Girl; Veronica Ganz; Fourteen; Bus Ride; Class Pictures.*

THIS PLACE HAS NO ATMOSPHERE
Paula Danziger
Delacorte, 1986
Even though Aurora loves her life on earth in the twenty-first century, her family is moving to the colony on the moon.
OTHER BOOKS: *The Cat Ate My Gymsuit; The Pistachio Prescription; There's A Bat in Bunk Five; The Divorce Express; It's An Aardvark-Eat-Turtle World.*

ANGEL SQUARE
Brian Doyle
Douglas & McIntyre, 1984
In this companion volume to "Up to Low," young Tommy, also known as The Shadow, sees Angel Square through new eyes when his best friend's father, a Jew, is beaten up.
OTHER BOOKS: *Up to Low; Hey, Dad; You Can Pick Me Up At Peggy's Cove.*

BLOSSOM CULP AND THE SLEEP OF DEATH
Richard Peck
Dell Publishing Co., 1987
Blossom Culp is the contact for the spirit of an ancient Egyptian princess. Enraged that her tomb has been disturbed and her mummy stolen, the Princess Sat-Hathor threatens poor Blossom with a certain curse, unless Blossom and Alexander can locate the missing mummy.
SERIES: *The Dreadful Future of Blossom Culp; Ghosts I Have Been; The Ghost Belonged to Me.*

OTHER BOOKS: *Princess Ashley; Representing Super Doll; Don't Look and It Won't Hurt; Secrets of the Shopping Mall; Through a Brief Darkness; Dreamland Lake; Are You in the House Alone?; Father Figure.*

THE WAR BETWEEN THE CLASSES
Gloria D. Miklowitz
Dell Publishing Co., 1986
Amy and Adam are involved in the "color game" at school, an experiment that's designed to make students aware of class and racial prejudices. The experiment threatens to alienate Amy, who is Japanese, from her friends.
OTHER BOOKS: *Close to the Edge; The Day the Senior Class Got Married; The Love Bombers; Did You Hear What Happened to Andrea?.*

ALAN AND THE ANIMAL KINGDOM
Isabelle Holland
Dell Publishing Co., 1977
The authorities who took care of orphan Alan MacGowan promised that Alan's pets would be well cared for, but they are put to sleep. When Alan's Aunt Jessie dies, he is determined to keep her death a secret in order to keep the officials away from him and his animal kingdom.
OTHER BOOKS: *Dinah and the Green Fat Kingdom; The Man Without a Face; Heads You Win, Tails I Lose.*

ISLAND OF THE BLUE DOLPHINS
Scott O'Dell
Houghton Mifflin, 1960
Karana, an Indian girl, spent eighteen years alone on a harsh rock known as the Island of San Nicholas. She must face battle with a pack of wild dogs, guard against sea-otter hunters, and maintain food supplies even when it means battling an octopus. Winner of the Newbery Medal.
SEQUEL: *Zia*
OTHER BOOKS: *The Black Pearl; Child of Fire; Sarah Bishop; Sing Down the Moon; The Hawk That Dare Not Hunt By Day.*

THE KEEPING DAYS
Norma Johnson
Ace Tempo, 1981
This is the first book in *The Keeping Days Saga.* The time is 1900 and the place is Yonkers, New York. This book records the events and thoughts of fourteen-year-old Fish Sterling in a Keeping Days journal.

OTHER BOOKS: *A Mustard Seed of Magic; The Sanctuary Tree; The Days of the Dragon's Seed; Myself and I.*

THE OUTSIDE SHOT
Walter Dean Myers
Dell Publishing Co., 1987
Lorrie Jackson's street smarts haven't prepared him for the pressures of the tough classes and the high-stakes of college basketball.
OTHER BOOKS: *Hoops*

HOLD FAST
Kevin Major
Dell Publishing Co., 1981
When Michael's parents are killed in a car accident he is forced to live with relatives far from his Newfoundland home. His uncle's tough discipline forces Michael to run away from home with his cousin Curtis. School Library Journal Best Book of the Year; Winner of The Canada Council Award; Winner of the Book of the Year Award from the Association of Canadian Children's Librarians.
OTHER BOOKS: *Far From Shore; Thirty-Six Exposures, Dear Bruce Springsteen.*

LITTLE, LITTLE
M.E. Kerr
Bantam Books, 1981
Little LaBelle and Sydney "The Roach" Cinnamon, have a lot in common, especially the fact that they're both less than 3 feet, 5 inches tall.
OTHER BOOKS: *Is That You Miss Blue?; Him She Loves; Dinky Hocker Shoots Smack; Gentlehands; Love is a Missing Person; What I Really Think of You; The Son of Someone Famous; I Stay Near You; Fell.*

Fiction for Mature Readers

Because of their well-developed reading abilities and mature interests, some adolescents may want to move into adult novels at this stage. However, many fine writers have written books especially for mature, young readers; these sophisticated, sensitive works of art deserve a place in their lives. Such books provide opportunities for these readers to focus on issues that affect them at their own emotional level, but that also stretch their minds and imaginations and present them with complicated and interlocking structures for deep learning as well.

DANCE ON MY GRAVE
Aidan Chambers
Harper & Row Publishers, 1983
The character Henry Spurly Robinson writes of a relationship that involves his own sexual identity in such a powerful way that at the end of it he is no longer the boy he was.
OTHER BOOKS: *Breaktime; Seal Secret; Now I Know.*

THE MACHINE-GUNNERS
Robert Westall
Puffin, 1975
When Charles McGill found the crashed German Heinkel, with a machine gun and all its ammunition intact, he had the power to enter both World War II and adulthood.
OTHER BOOKS: *The Scarecrows; Fathom Five; Break of Dark; The Devil On the Road; The Wind Eye; Urn Burial.*

THE MOON AND THE FACE
Patricia A. McKillip
Berkley, 1986
In this sequel to *Moon-flash* the people of the planet Riverworld possess the power of dreaming the future and Kyreol discovers that her home world will host an interstellar civilization.
SERIES: *Moon-flash*
OTHER BOOKS: *The Forgotten Beasts of Eld; Stepping from the Shadows; An Heir of Sea & Fire; The Riddle-Master of Hed; Harpist & the Wind.*

THE SECRET DIARY OF ADRIAN MOLE AGED 13 3/4
Sue Townsend
Methuen, 1983
This satirical journal chronicles the humorous pains of family life and of growing up.
SEQUEL: *The Growing Pains of Adrian Mole*

SMITH
Leon Garfield
Puffin, 1968
Smith is a 12-year-old ruffian who grubs a living from the streets of a Dickensian London. The book contains descriptions of tavern and prison life, and adventures with highwaymen, robbers, and traitors.
OTHER BOOKS: *The Night of the Comet: A Comedy of Courtship featuring Bostock and Harris; Mr. Corbett's Ghost; Footsteps; Jack Holborn.*

A STRANGER CAME ASHORE
Mollie Hunter
Piccolo Pan, 1975
When Finn Learson emerges as the only survivor of a fierce storm
and shipwreck, the Shetland Islanders begin to wonder if Finn could
be one of the mysterious Selkie Folk, seal-like creatures who become
human when they come ashore.
OTHER BOOKS: *A Sound of Chariots; The Walking Stones; The Kelpie's
Pearls; Cat, Herself; The Haunted Mountain; The Ghosts of Glencoe; I'll
Go My Own Way; The Third Eye.*

SWEET WHISPERS, BROTHER RUSH
Virginia Hamilton
Avon Camelot, 1983
Having the responsibility of looking after her retarded brother and
taking care of a household basically on her own, Teresa comes to
terms with her brother's death, her mother's weaknesses, and her
own vulnerability. A Newbery Honor Book.
OTHER BOOKS: *The House of Dies Drear; Mystery of Drear House; M.C.
Higgins, the Great; Dustland; The Planet of Junior Brown; The Gathering;
Justice and Her Brothers; Zeely; Arilla Sun Down.*

TO THE WILD SKY
Ivan Southall
Puffin, 1971
A party of six children sets off by plane to visit a sheep station in
New South Wales. When disaster strikes the pilot, fourteen-year-old
Gerald takes over the controls, but once landed, the group faces a
more terrifying situation of survival.
SEQUEL: *A City Out of Sight*
OTHER BOOKS: *Hill's End; Finn's Folly; Ash Road; King of the Sticks; The
Golden Goose; The Long Nightwatch.*

WALKABOUT
James Vance Marshall
Peacock, 1983
An adolescent girl and her young brother are left after a
confrontation with their father in the Australian outback, miles away
from anywhere. A young aborigine attempts to help the two
children.

Themes

Young adolescents have common interests that are revealed in their reading choices. These themes reflect their developing lives and their questions about their place in society. While the context may be fantastical, the issues are real, and the problems faced are similar to those of the adolescent readers. The analogies and the metaphors used by the authors allow the readers safe mirrors with which to examine their concerns. A particular novel will include several overlapping themes, but the books have been grouped according to the major issue that affects the characters.

Themes: Relationships

EXIT BARNEY MCGEE
Claire Mackay
Scholastic-TAB, 1979
When his mother has a baby, Barney feels that he is no longer needed. He runs away to meet his father who himself had run out on his family.
OTHER BOOKS: *The Minerva Program; One Proud Summer.*

ANGEL FACE
Norma Klein
Ballantine Books, 1985
Everyone calls Jason Angel Face. His parents are splitting up and he is falling in love for the first time.
OTHER BOOKS: *Love and Other Euphemisms; Mom, The Wolf Man and Me; Robbie and the Leap Year Blues; Confessions of an Only Child; The Queen of the Whatifs; Bizou.*

THE MOONLIGHT MAN
Paula Fox
Bradbury Press, 1986
Catherine's father, Harry Ames, is a traveler and a drunk. He phoned three weeks late, after school ended, and told her he'd rented a small house near the sea for a month, and invites her to spend the time with him.
OTHER BOOKS: *The Stone-faced Boy; Blowfish Live in the Sea; One-Eyed Cat; How Many Miles To Babylon?; The Slave Dancer.*

IOU'S
Ouida Sebestyen
Atlantic Monthly Press, 1982
Thirteen-year-old Stowe Garrett and his mother, Annie, depend on monthly checks from his grandfather who walked out on Annie when she really needed him, just as Stowe's own father walked out on him.
OTHER BOOKS: *Words By Heart; Far From Home.*

THE TRUE STORY OF LILLI STUBECK
James Aldridge
Puffin, 1985
The down and out Stubeck family arrived in the Australian country town of St. Helen, but when they left, it was without their wilful daughter, Lilli, who was "bought" by the wealthy Miss Dalgleish. Australian Book of the Year Winner.

DICEY'S SONG
Cynthia Voigt
Fawcett Juniper, 1984
This sequel to *Homecoming* continues the story of Dicey Tillerman, a determined young girl who brought her brothers and sisters to safety at Gram's house when their mother abandoned them. Winner of the Newbery Medal.
SERIES: *Homecoming; The Callender Papers; A Solitary Blue.*
OTHER BOOKS: *Jackaroo; Building Blocks; Izzy, Willy Nilly; The Runner; Tell Me if the Lovers are Losers; Come a Stranger.*

GOODNIGHT, MR. TOM
Michelle Magorian
Puffin, 1981
Young Willie Beech is evacuated to the country as Britain stands on the brink of the Second World War. Willie is under the care of Tom Oakley, a bitter bachelor. Winner of the Guardian Children's Fiction Prize.
OTHER BOOKS: *Back Home*

ALL TOGETHER NOW
Sue Ellen Bridgers
Bantam Books, 1979
Casey was spending the summer with her grandmother, Jane, while her father was off fighting. She made a friend of Dwayne, a grown up man whose mind was forever frozen in childhood, and since

Dwayne did not like girls, she lied and told him she was a boy.
OTHER BOOKS: *Permanent Connections; Home Before Dark; Notes for Another Life.*

A DAY NO PIGS WOULD DIE
Robert Newton Peck
Dell Publishing Co., 1972
Set among Shaker farmers in Vermont during the 1920's, this story deals with the narrator's coming of age at thirteen, and describes his special relationship with his father.
OTHER BOOKS: *Fawn; Millie's Boy; Justice Lion; Spanish Hoof; Kirk's Law.*

JACOB HAVE I LOVED
Katherine Paterson
Thomas Y. Crowell, 1981
Growing up on a tiny Chesapeake Bay island in the early 1940's, angry Louise reveals how her sister, Caroline, robbed her of her hopes for schooling, her friends, her mother, and even her name.
OTHER BOOKS: *Bridge to Terabithia; The Great Gilly Hopkins; Come Sing, Jimmy Jo.*

Themes: Science Fiction/Fantasy

THE CITY UNDER GROUND
Suzanne Martel
Douglas & McIntyre, 1982
It is the year 3000. In the underground city, Luke discovers a doorway to the outside and ventures into a world devastated by nuclear attack that occurred one thousand years in the past.
OTHER BOOKS: *The King's Daughter*

HIGH WAY HOME
Nicholas Fisk
Puffin, 1976
A millionaire's daughter, Baba, rich Barry, and awkward Rupert are marooned on a sinister island. In their need to get off the island, the characters are free for the first time to see and value each other as real people.
OTHER BOOKS: *You Remember Me; Grinny; Space Hostages; Trillions; A Rag, A Bone and a Hank of Hair.*

THE ENNEAD
Jan Mark
Puffin, 1980
Erato is a bleak planet with a corrupt government. All behavior is rigidly controlled. Isaac plays the games and sticks to all the rules, although through scheming and bribing. One day he makes a fatal mistake and rescues a young sculptress from another planet.
OTHER BOOKS: *Handles; Thunder and Lightnings.*

ARCHER'S GOON
Diana Wynne Jones
Greenwillow Books, 1984
The Goon moves into the Sykes's house, and when he refuses to budge, thirteen-year-old Howard learns startling information about his family and the seven wizards who run the town.
OTHER BOOKS: *Dogsbody; Witch Week; Power of Three; The Magicians of Caprona; Charmed Life; The Homeward Bounders.*

THE WHITE MOUNTAINS
John Christopher
Collier Books, 1970
In the next century, the world is enslaved by Tripods. Will Parker sets out from his English village to the White Mountains where men still live in freedom.
OTHER BOOKS IN THE TRILOGY: *The City of Gold and Lead; The Pool of Fire.*
OTHER BOOKS: *(Trilogy) The Prince in Waiting; Beyond the Burning Lands; The Sword of the Spirits; (Trilogy) Fireball; New Found Land; Dragon Dance; The Guardians; Wild Jack; Empty World.*

THE DREAM CATCHER
Monica Hughes
Methuen, 1986
This sequel to *Devil on My Back,* is set inside the protective Dome of Ark Three.
SERIES: *Devil on My Back*
OTHER BOOKS: *(Trilogy) The Keeper of the Isis Light; The Guardian of Isis; The Isis Pedlar; The Tomorrow City; Space Trap; Beckoning Lights; Crisis on Conshelf Ten; Ring-Rise, Ring-Set; Sandwriter.*

Z FOR ZACHARIAH
Robert C. O'Brien
Dell Publishing Co., 1974
In a world of the future there is no sign of anyone being alive except

for Anna Burden. Anna sees the smoke of a campfire coming closer each day, and she meets John R. Loomis wearing a safe-suit, the only one in existence. Anna was glad to see another human being but wonders if it was really a good thing that Loomis had come. Edgar Award Winner from Mystery Writers of America.

DRAGON'S BLOOD
Jane Yolen
Delacorte Press, 1982
Jakkin, a bond boy who works as a keeper in a dragon nursery on the planet Austar IV, secretly trains a fighting pit dragon of his own in hopes of winning his freedom.
OTHER BOOKS: *Heart's Blood*

A GAME OF DARK
William Mayne
Jonathon Cape, 1971
Fourteen-year-old Donald Jackson struggles with his stern, fundamentalist parents while his fantasy life puts him in battle as a medieval squire fighting the monstrous Worm.
OTHER BOOKS: *A Swarm in May; A Grass Rope; The Jersey Shore; The Changeling; Max's Dream.*

OVER SEA, UNDER STONE
Susan Cooper
Puffin, 1968
A holiday in Logres turns up an ancient map that leads to adventure and a search for a buried Grail.
SERIES: *The Dark is Rising; Greenwitch; The Grey King; Silver on the Tree.*

THE HERO AND THE CROWN
Robin McKinley
Greenwillow Books, 1984
Aerin's destiny was to be the true hero who would wield the power of the Blue sword in the realm of Hillfolk. Winner of the 1985 Newbery Medal.
SEQUEL: *The Blue Sword*

THE DEVIL'S CHILDREN
Peter Dickinson
Little, Brown & Company, 1970
In a future time when people hate machines and have returned to a fearful primitive way of life, a London girl, Nicky, who has lost her

parents, joins a group of wandering nomads who become the only family she has.
SERIES: *Heartsease; The Weathermonger.*
OTHER BOOKS: *The Blue Hawk; Tulku; The Dancing Bear; Annerton Pit.*

A WIZARD OF EARTHSEA
Ursula Le Guin
Penguin, 1975
The first title in Le Guin's classic fantasy, *The Earthsea Trilogy*, which deals with the education, both spiritual and magical, of the young wizard Ged.
OTHER BOOKS IN THE TRILOGY: *The Tombs of Atuan; The Farthest Shore.*

DRAGONSONG
Anne McCaffrey
Bantam Books, 1977
Girls are forbidden to sing on Pern. Menooly, whose greatest love is music, runs away and befriends a group of fire lizards, finally realizing her dream of becoming a musician.
SERIES: *Dragonsinger; Dragondrums.*

Themes: Mystery and Adventure

THE SILVER SWORD
Ian Seraillier
Puffin, 1975
When the Nazis invaded Poland, men and women were carried off to prison camps and children left alone, homeless, to fend for themselves. Jan and the three Balackis children survived the war, then made their own way from Poland to Germany and into Switzerland.

LOCKED IN TIME
Lois Duncan
Dell Publishing Co., 1985
When Nore Robbins spends the summer with her father and new stepmother on their Louisiana plantation, she enters a world of nightmares.
OTHER BOOKS: *Daughters of Eve; Summer of Fear; Killing Mr. Griffin; Ransom; I Know What You Did Last Summer.*

NOAH'S CASTLE
John Rowe Townsend
Harper & Row Publishers, 1976
When Father suddenly announces that the family will be moving into a new house, he starts to stockpile food and won't allow anyone to visit the house.
OTHER BOOKS: *The Summer People; Gumble's Yard; Good Night, Prof, Dear; The Visitors; The Invader; The Islanders; Hill's Edge; Kate and the Revolution; Dan Alone; Cloudy-Bright.*

FROZEN FIRE
James Houston
Puffin, 1979
A gripping tale of life in the North. Mathew and his eskimo friend Kayak find themselves separated from Mathew's father and his pilot. The two boys show enormous strength and courage and use Eskimo survival techniques to prevent a hideous death.
OTHER BOOKS: *The White Archer; Ice Swords; Black Diamonds; Long Claws.*

ZED
Rosemary Harris
Magnet Books, 1982
Thomas is a hostage who is held at gun-point by a group of fanatic terrorists who will stop at nothing to achieve their aims. Thomas learns about his father, but most of all about himself.
OTHER BOOKS: *The Seal-Singing*

ON THE EDGE
Gillian Cross
Puffin, 1987
In this suspense story, Tug is kidnapped by a strange man and woman who bring him to a remote Derbyshire cottage.
OTHER BOOKS: *The Iron Way; The Demon Headmaster.*

HOUSE OF STAIRS
William Sleator
Scholastic, 1981
Orphans Peter, Lola, Blossom, Abigail, and Oliver find themselves thrust into a stark white room—no walls, no ceiling, no floor, only staircases twisting in every direction as far as the eye can see.
OTHER BOOKS: *Blackbriar; The Green Futures of Tycho; Fingers; Singularity; Into the Dream.*

THE SNARKOUT BOYS AND THE AVOCADO OF DEATH
Daniel M. Pinkwater
Lothrop, Lee & Shepard, 1982
A cast of odd characters plan to save the earth from alien space invaders.
SERIES: *The Snarkout Boys and the Baconburg Horror*
OTHER BOOKS: *Lizard Music; The Last Guru.*

THE HAUNTING
Margaret Mahy
Magnet, 1984
In this psychological thriller, members of his dead mother's family all seem aware that there is something special about Barney, though everyone seems too frightened to say what it might be. Carnegie Medal Winner.
OTHER BOOKS: *The Changeover; Aliens in the Family; The Tricksters.*

PLAYING BEATIE BOW
Ruth Park
Puffin, 1980
Children in the park played the game Beatie Bow for the thrill of scaring themselves. Abigail Kirk ends up in Victorian Sydney, where she escapes the problems of home only to find herself trapped in time with new problems to face. Winner of the Australian Children's Book of the Year Award.

Themes: Historical Fiction

MY BROTHER SAM IS DEAD
James Lincoln Collier, Christopher Collier
Scholastic, 1974
Sam is a part of the new American Revolutionary Army. Most people are loyal supporters of the English king, especially Tim and Sam's father. Tim knows he'll have to make a choice between fighting his father on one side, and fighting his brother on the other. A Newbery Honor Book.
OTHER BOOKS: *(Trilogy) Jump Ship to Freedom; War Comes to Willy Freeman; Who is Carrie?; The Bloody Country; The Winter Hero.*

THE FIGHTING GROUND
Avi
Harper & Row Publishers, 1987
In 1778, when the tolling bell breaks the quiet of the New Jersey

countryside, Jonathan, a thirteen-year-old, is ready to fight the British, and in the next twenty-four hours, his understanding of war and life is changed forever. Winner of the Scott O'Dell Award for historical fiction.
OTHER BOOKS: *Night Journeys; Encounter at Easton.*

TRANSPORT 7-41-R
T. Degens
Laurel Leaf, 1974
An old man and a dead woman were to become a young girl's responsibility on a long and treacherous journey aboard Transport 7-41-R to the bombed-out city of Cologne.
OTHER BOOKS: *The Visit; Friends.*

DAYS OF TERROR
Barbara Smucker
Clarke, Irwin & Co., 1976
Set in 1917, this story of the mass exodus of Mennonites to Canada from Russia during the Russian revolution is seen through the eyes of ten-year-old Peter Neufeld.
OTHER BOOKS: *Amish Adventure; Underground to Canada; White Mist.*

SHADOW IN HAWTHORN BAY
Janet Lunn
Lester & Orpen Dennys, 1986
In 1815, Mairi Urquhart is mysteriously called from her family home in the Scottish highlands to cross the seas to the North American colony her cousin Duncan and his family emigrated to four years before. When she finally reaches the little settlement on the shores of Lake Ontario near Kingston, it is only to find that Duncan has died and his family has returned to Scotland.
OTHER BOOKS: *The Root Cellar*

THE WILD CHILDREN
Felice Holman
Puffin, 1985
This adventure depicts the resilience and courage of a group of wild children—bezprizovni (children left homeless after the Russian Revolution)—who band together in packs in order to survive the miserable conditions that surround them.

ONE PROUD SUMMER
Marsha Hewitt and Claire Mackay
Women's Educational Press, 1981

In the 1946 strike against Montreal Cottons the mill workers of
Valleyfield, Quebec are pitted against a national company, the
provincial police, and the Catholic Church. The story is seen through
the eyes of 13-year-old Lucie LaPlante, who has to quit school to
work in the mill.

THE QUARTER-PIE WINDOW
Marianne Brandis
Firefly Books, 1985
This award-winning sequel to *The Tinderbox* follows Emma
Anderson's life in the 1830's in the city of New York. Emma
struggles for herself and her younger brother under the stern
guardianship of Mrs. McPhail. The quarter-pie window in Emma's
room lets her view the world outside.
SEQUEL: *The Tinderbox*

A GATHERING OF DAYS: A NEW ENGLAND GIRL'S JOURNAL
Joan Blos
Charles Scribner's Sons, 1985
Following the birth of an infant son, Catherine Hall's mother died.
Her father decides to remarry, forcing Catherine to face painful
changes. The story is told in the form of a survival set in New
England. Winner of the Newbery Medal.
OTHER BOOKS: *Brothers of the Heart*

MIDNIGHT IS A PLACE
Joan Aiken
Puffin, 1974
Two orphans, Lucas, thirteen, and waif-like Anne-Marie, are cast
down from privilege to hard times in this story of a nineteenth
century carpet mill.
OTHER BOOKS: *The Wolves of Willoughby Chase; Black Hearts in Battersea;
The Whispering Mountain; The Faithless Lollybird; Nightbirds on
Nantucket; The Stolen Lake.*

THE LIGHT BEYOND THE FOREST
Rosemary Sutcliff
Bodley Head, 1979
The story is concerned with the Quest of the Fellowship of the
Round Table for the Holy Grail, the sacred dish from which the Last
Supper was served, and which prophecies claim would only be
approached by the world's most perfect knight.
OTHER BOOKS: *Flame-Colored Taffeta; Song for a Dark Queen; Frontier
Wolf; Sun Horse, Moon Horse; Bonnie Dundee; Eagle of the Ninth.*

Theme: Issues

IT'S TOO LATE FOR SORRY
Emily Hanlon
Dell Publishing Co., 1981
Rachel wanted to bring Harold Havermeyer, a retarded teenager,
into the mainstream, creating trouble for her boyfriend Kenny.
OTHER BOOKS: *Circle Home; The Swing; The Wing and the Flame.*

THE BUMBLEBEE FLIES AWAY
Robert Cormier
Dell Publishing Co., 1977
A story of a hospice for teenagers who may be dying, where the
courage of the young people transcends their conditions.
OTHER BOOKS: *The Chocolate War; Beyond the Chocolate War; I Am the
Cheese; After the First Death.*

HEY DUMMY
Kin Platt
Dell Publishing Co., 1971
Twelve-year-old Neil befriends Alan, a brain-damaged boy of
thirteen. As the friendship grows, Neil comes to understand the
plight of the helpless boy who is taunted by his cruel peers.
OTHER BOOKS: *The Ape Inside Me; Chloris and the Freaks; Chloris and the
Creeps; Chloris and the Weirdos.*

HUNTER IN THE DARK
Monica Hughes
Avon Books, 1984
Just before his birthday, Mike Rankin, a successful sixteen-year-old
athlete, suddenly passes out while playing in a school basketball
game. It is evident that he has a very serious disease which his
parents will not talk about.
OTHER BOOKS: *Log Jam; My Name is Paula Popowich.*

WATER SKY
Jean Craighead George
Irwin Publishing, 1987
Lincoln had made the long trip from Massachusetts to Barrow,
Alaska, to find his Uncle Jack to help save the bowhead whale from
extinction.
OTHER BOOKS: *My Side of the Mountain; Julie of the Wolves; Hook a Fish,
Catch a Mountain.*

I AM DAVID
Anne Holm
Methuen, 1963
David, a boy from a concentration camp, travels across Europe knowing that any moment the authorities may catch him.
OTHER BOOKS: *North to Freedom*

DOGSONG
Gary Paulsen
Puffin, 1987
This story charts the physical and spiritual journey of a teenage Inuit boy who shuns the modern ways of his village.
OTHER BOOKS: *Dancing Carl; Tracker; Sentries.*

BROTHER IN THE LAND
Robert Swindells
Puffin, 1985
Danny and his young brother Ben have come through the atomic holocaust alive, where survival depends on being able to live on your wits, fighting to protect home and family. Winner of the Other Award.

TUNNEL VISION
Fran Arrick
Dell Publishing Co., 1980
Fifteen-year-old Anthony Hame commits suicide, and leaves behind his family, friends, and girlfriend, who all must question their own parts in Anthony's decision to take his own life.
OTHER BOOKS: *Steffie Can't Come Out to Play; Chernowitz!; God's Radar.*

NIGHT KITES
M.E. Kerr
Harper & Row Publishers, 1986
Seventeen-year-old Jim's relationship with his family and friends change when his older brother reveals he has AIDS.
OTHER BOOKS: *Gentlehands*

SUMMER OF MY GERMAN SOLDIER
Bette Greene
Bantam Books, 1981
When the German prisoners arrive at the POW Camp outside Jenkinsville, Arkansas, Patty, a twelve-year-old girl, develops a dangerous friendship with a German soldier during World War II, when patriotic feeling was running high.

SEQUEL: *Morning Is a Long Time Coming*
OTHER BOOKS: *Them That Glitter and Them That Don't*

WINNERS
Mary-Ellen Lang Collura
Western Producer Prairie Books, 1984
Fifteen-year-old Jordy Threebears had lived in eleven foster homes.
Now he was returning to the Ash Creek Reserve to live with a
grandfather and the years of bitterness prove difficult for Jordy to
overcome until he receives the gift of a wild horse. 1984 National
Chapter IODE Book Award. 1985 Young Adult Canadian Book
Award.

MOSES BEECH
Ian Strachan
Puffin, 1983
Peter Simpson was on the run from his layabout father, and old
Moses Beech offered him shelter in his isolated cottage. Moses's way
of life wasn't able to survive this sudden intrusion. Winner of the
first Observer/Rank Organization fiction prize.

ROLL OF THUNDER, HEAR MY CRY
Mildred D. Taylor
Bantam Books, 1979
This is the story of Cassie Logan, a girl raised by a family
determined not to surrender their independence or humanity simply
because they are black. Newbery Award Winner, 1977.
OTHER BOOKS: *Let the Circle be Unbroken; Song of the Trees.*

Themes: Biography

SOMETHING FOR JOEY
Richard E. Peck
Bantam Books, 1978
The story of courage and love between John Cappeletti, winner of
the Heisman Trophy for outstanding college football player, and his
younger brother, Joey, who suffered from leukemia.

KAREN
Maria Killilea
Laurel Leaf, 1983
A story of human courage, patience, and triumph as told by the
mother of a handicapped girl.
SEQUEL: *With Love From Karen*

BRIAN'S SONG
William Blinn
Bantam Books, 1972
Gale Sayers and Brian Piccolo came from different parts of the
country and competed fiercely for the same job. One was white; the
other black. This story describes how they came to know each other,
fight each other, and help each other.

TO BE A SLAVE
Julius Lester
Dial Books, 1968
Told through their own words and provided with a comentary by
the author, this book depicts the conditions of slavery with first
person accounts. A Newbery Honor book.

THE EDUCATION OF LITTLE TREE
Forrest Carter
Dell Publishing Co., 1981
This autobiographical story of Forrest Carter's boyhood illuminates
the mystical relationship between the Indian and his land, and
illustrates the frequent misunderstandings between the Indian and
the white man.

THE ALPINE PATH
L.M. Montgomery
Fitzhenry & Whiteside, 1987
Lucy Maud Montgomery, the creator of *Anne of Green Gables*, wrote
this autobiographical memoir in the middle of her career.

HOMESICK: MY OWN STORY
Jean Fritz
Dell Publishing Co., 1984
A memoir of Fritz's missionary childhood beside the Yangtze River
in turbulent pre-revolutionary China. Winner of a Newbery Award.
SEQUEL: *China Homecoming*
OTHER BOOKS: *And Then What Happened, Paul Revere?*

GOING SOLO
Roald Dahl
Harcourt Brace Jovanovich, 1986
Master storyteller Dahl shares some comic and terrifying
autobiographical experiences in this companion to *Boy*.
OTHER BOOKS: *Boy*

ME ME ME ME ME: NOT A NOVEL
M.E. Kerr
Signet Vista, 1984
These biographical stories from M.E. Kerr's past are reflected in the
characters and situations from her novels.

THE DIARY OF ANNE FRANK
Anne Frank
Pan Books, 1954
Thirteen-year-old Anne Frank went into hiding in the sealed-off back
rooms of an Amsterdam office building in 1942 when the Nazi
invaders intensified their persecution of Jews.

Classics

Books for young adolescents that have stood the test of time are
labelled classics. Experienced readers still can enjoy them, although
adults must be careful not to force their love of classics on
youngsters who are not interested in or prepared for them. As
reading tastes and writing styles alter, readers may make alternate
choices or come to these books at another time. The classics listed
are only representative of the numbers of books available to
independent readers; contemporary writers will no doubt be
included on future lists.

LITTLE WOMEN
Louisa M. Alcott
1868; Puffin, 1953
Meg, Jo, Beth and Amy struggle against their poverty with
irresistible charm and good nature.
SEQUELS: *Good Wives; Jo's Boys; Little Men.*

THE ADVENTURES OF TOM SAWYER
Mark Twain
1876; Penguin, 1987
Mark Twain's hymn to the fantastic world of boyhood adventure.
OTHER BOOKS: *The Prince and the Pauper; Huckleberry Finn; A
Connecticut Yankee in King Arthur's Court.*

TREASURE ISLAND
Robert Louis Stevenson
1883; Bantam Books, 1981
Jim Hawkins had no idea when he picked up the oilskin packet from
Captain Flint's sea chest that there lay the key to untold wealth—a

treasure map. Then Jim sails on the Hispaniola as cabin-boy with the awesome Long John Silver, and embarks on an adventure full of excitement and suspense.

OTHER BOOKS: *Kidnapped*

CALL OF THE WILD
Jack London
Bantam Books, 1963
The story of Buck, a dog stolen from his home and thrust into the merciless life of the Arctic north to endure hardship, bitter cold, and the savage lawlessness of man and beast.

OTHER BOOKS: *The White Fang*

JOURNEY TO THE CENTRE OF THE EARTH
Jules Verne
1864; Puffin Classics, 1965
Verne takes the reader on a journey to solve a secret message, written in runes. Professor Von Hardwigs, chemist, philosopher, mineralogist, set to work and finally decoded the message which read: "Descend into the crater of yocul of Sneffels which the shade of Scartarios caresses, before the Kalends of July, audacious traveller, and you will reach the centre of the earth."

OTHER BOOKS: *Twenty Thousand Leagues Under the Sea; Around the World in Eighty Days; From Earth to the Moon.*

THE LORD OF THE RINGS
J.R.R. Tolkien
Unwin Paperback, 1974
Tolkien created a new mythology in an invented world which has proved timeless in its appeal.

OTHER BOOKS: *(Trilogy) The Fellowship of the Ring; The Two Towers; The Return of the King; The Hobbit.*

JANE EYRE
Charlotte Bronte
1847; many editions
Jane Eyre is about a young girl's awakening to life and to love. Readers see her grow from a shy schoolgirl to a spirited young governess who does not let class barriers keep her from falling in love with her employer, the arrogant, brooding Mr. Rochester.

Information Books

Young adolescents are able to make use of information books for personal projects, for school assignments, and for general interest. It is important that they recognize the value of these reading materials, and that they seek them out in school and public libraries as well as at book stores. The range of information books is endless, from how-to manuals to expensive coffee table books. The suggested list only partially covers the great variety of materials available to today's readers.

CANADA IN SPACE
Lydia Dotto
Irwin Publishing, 1987
A close-up look at the Canadian involvement in the manned space program. Dotto describes all aspects of the program, including manned space travel, the shuttle program, and the international space station.

THE CIVIL RIGHTS MOVEMENT IN AMERICA
Patricia and Frederick McKissak
Children's Press, 1986
This book is mainly devoted to the struggle of Black Americans for equality from 1865 to the present.

DEAR DOCTOR: TEENAGERS ASK ABOUT . . .
Dr. Saul Levine and Dr. Kathleen Wilcox
Kids Can Press, 1986
Teenagers have been asking the experts questions at a newspaper's "Youth Clinic" for 13 years. The authors have published a book of the most representative letters and replies from their syndicated column. *Dear Doctor . . .* puts teens' problems into perspective.

TEEN SUICIDE
Janet Kolehmainen and Sandra Handwerk
Lerner Publications, 1986
A discussion of teen suicide, the second leading cause of death in adolescents and young adults.

THEY SOUGHT A NEW WORLD
William Kurelek; Additional Text by Margaret S. Engelhart
Tundra Books, 1985
This book was created at the request of European publishers who felt Kurulek's paintings told in human terms, graphically and unforgettably, the story of immigration and life in the New World.
OTHER BOOKS: *A Prairie Boy's Winter; A Prairie Boy's Summer; Lumberjack, A Northern Nativity.*

UNDERGROUND
David Macaulay
Houghton Mifflin, 1976

Macaulay describes some of man's more modern accomplishments and offers a unique perspective of the subterranean. He provides on-the-scene observation of manholes beneath the busiest of city streets, subway tunnels, building sites, and architects' plans.
OTHER BOOKS: *Cathedral; City; Pyramid; Castle.*

Read Aloud/Tell Aloud

Young adolescents still need to be read to and to listen to stories being told. When adults share literature aloud, they reveal their literary choices, demonstrate their appreciation and taste, and bring alive the words on the page for the listeners. The impact of adults who read and tell stories aloud will affect what young people choose to read as well as influence their feelings about what is read and about those who read. If careful choices are made, the teenagers can be exposed to books they might not choose or are unable to read on their own. They can hear a wide range of options—excerpts from new novels, books from other cultures and countries, sections from novels for adults, folktales told aloud, and poems interpreted orally.

THE APPRENTICES
Leon Garfield
Penguin, 1978
These twelve stories link the destinies of twelve grimy, wretched but enthusiastic London apprentices through a year in their lives.

A CHANCE CHILD
Jill Paton Walsh
Avon Books, 1978
Creep, an abused child, takes a river journey into another time, nineteenth century England. As he travels from the present to the past, he discovers a world where children are treated as harshly as himself.
OTHER BOOKS: *Goldengrove; Fireweed; Unleaving; The Dolphin Crossing; A Parcel of Patterns; Children of the Fox; The Butty Boy.*

CONJURE TALES
Charles W. Chesnutt; retold by Ray Anthony Shepard; ill. John Ross and Clare Romano
E.P. Dutton Books, 1973
These Afro-American short stories of conjuring and voodoo appeared around 1890, the work of a black lawyer and writer.

THE GOLDEN SHADOW
Leon Garfield and Edward Blishen; ill. Charles Keeping
Longman Young Books, 1973

The rivalries and presences of the Greek gods pervade this book. Heracles's adventures form the heart of this book and cover the whole range of human experience.
SERIES: *The God Beneath the Sea*

THE LITTLE PRINCE
Antoine de Saint Exupéry; translated from the French by Katherine Woods
Harcourt Brace and World, 1971
Pride ruined the Little Prince's world and started him on travels that brought him to Earth, where he learned the secret of what is really important in life.

THE OWL SERVICE
Alan Garner
William Collins Sons, 1973
Three young people in a Welsh valley find themselves playing parts assigned to them by ancient myth. A power rises between and around them, which explodes in a wild climax. Winner of the Carnegie Medal in 1967.
OTHER BOOKS: *Tom Fobble's Day; The Aimer Gate; Red Shift.*

WAITING TO WALTZ
Cynthia Rylant; ill. Stephen Gammell
Bradbury Press, 1984
Cynthia Rylant's portrait of a childhood flows from image to image to create a world through carefully crafted poems.

Picture Books for Sharing

Many picture books have been created especially for young adolescent readers. The words and the pictures blend together into a special art form that allows a shared reading experience by groups, as the words can be read aloud and the pictures viewed at the same time. All types and styles of art can be used in creating the pictures, all manners of writing can be used in creating the text. The medium allows for a variety of concepts to be explored as well. Teenage readers can also experience picture books by preparing them for reading to younger audiences, reliving their own experiences and reflecting on the books they once loved.

BEOWULF
Kevin Crossley-Holland; ill. Charles Keeping
Oxford University Press, 1982
An illustrated version of the original myth, Beowulf.
OTHER BOOKS: *Sammy Streetsinger; The Highwayman; The Wedding Guest.*

THE CREMATION OF SAM MCGEE
Robert W. Service; paintings by Ted Harrison
Kids Can Press, 1986
Service's most famous poem has been illustrated by Ted Harrison.

THE DANCING TIGERS
Russell Hoban; ill. David Gentleman
Jonathon Cape, 1979
A Raja learns that the tigers will accept their fate only if hunted in traditional ways.

THE HIGHWAYMAN
Alfred Noyes; ill. Charles Mikolaycak
Lothrop, Lee & Shepard, 1983
Noyes's ballad about the highwayman and Bess, the landlord's daughter, with Mikolaycak's theatrical illustrations.

THE HOCKEY SWEATER
Roch Carrier
Tundra Books, 1984
A mix-up in a catalogue order results in the delivery of a Toronto Maple Leafs sweater, instead of a Montreal Canadiens sweater, to a young Maurice (Rocket) Richard fan.

THE MYSTERIES OF HARRIS BURDICK
Chris Van Allsburg
Houghton Mifflin, 1984
Fourteen pictures with accompanying captions created by a fictitious author create a mystery to be solved in the reader's imagination.
OTHER BOOKS: *The Stranger; Jumanji; The Wreck of the Zephyr; The Garden of Abdul Gasazi; The Polar Express.*

ROSE BLANCHE
Christophe Gallaz and Roberto Innocenti; ill. Roberto Innocenti
Creative Education, 1985
A grim picture book depicting a young girl's response to a prison camp of the Holocaust.

THE SEA PEOPLE
Jörg Müller & Jörg Steiner
Victor Gollancz, 1982
A tale of two islands and the fate that befalls them when the greedy king of the Greater Island gives way to his selfishness.

SNOW WHITE IN NEW YORK
Fiona French
Oxford University Press, 1986
A satire on the famous fairy tale, set in the thirties, with Art Deco drawings by the author.
OTHER BOOKS: *Future Story*

Myth, Legend and Folktale

Traditionally, myths are studied during adolescence, but the readers should have met many tales in their reading lives, as preparation for interpreting mythology. It is important that young people experience a variety of myth and legend, from creation stories to classical mythology. As well, folktale can be presented in a variety of forms—picture books, epic poems, tall tales, novels, including different versions of the same story.

EXODUS
adapted by Miriam Chaikin; ill. Charles Mikolaycak
Holiday House, 1987
The author remains faithful to the Biblical text, retelling the story of Moses leading his enslaved people out of Egypt. Mikolaycak interprets the story with illustrations that reflect careful research into ancient Egypt.

KING ARTHUR AND HIS KNIGHTS
Anthony Mockler; ill. Nick Harris
Oxford University Press, 1984
In his new version of the stories of a king and his knights, Mockler depicts the world of King Arthur—a world of forests and fountains, castles and tournaments, giants and wild beasts, mystery and enchantment. The stories are divided into three parts, The Book of Merlin, The Book of Knights, and The Book of Doom.

THE LEGEND OF ODYSSEUS
Peter Connolly
Oxford University Press, 1986
Connolly's adaptation of Homer's famous story is informed and enhanced by a detailed archaeological presentation of the Greek and Trojan way of life at the time of Odysseus.

Collections

For many young readers, anthologies present successful reading experiences, with short stories written by an author or collected thematically by an editor. Often a particular interest can be met with a concentrated focus in a collection. These stories can be read aloud to individuals or groups.

SIXTEEN
edited by Donald R. Gallo
Dell Publishing Co., 1984
Sixteen stories written especially for this collection by today's popular writers for teenagers, with themes of hope and hate, love and death, despair and joy.

BADGER ON THE BARGE
Jannie Howker
Puffin Books, 1987
Howker creates a gallery of characters in these five stories, each of which describes a significant encounter between two people— one young, one old.

WHO'S AFRAID? AND OTHER STRANGE STORIES
Philippa Pearce
Viking Kestrel, 1986
These stories explore the possibilities of the supernatural— the spine-chiller, and the blood-curdler.
OTHER BOOKS: *The Shadow Cage and Other Tales of the Supernatural*

SHADES OF DARK
Aidan Chambers
Penguin, 1986
Chambers' collection of eight original ghost stories.
OTHER BOOKS: *A Quiver of Ghosts*

8 PLUS 1
Robert Cormier
Bantam Books, 1982
These nine stories probe the feelings and reactions of people in life's trying situations.

Poetry

During these years, some young people find poetry of particular interest with its emotional appeal, its unusual forms, its brevity, and its succinctness. With so many new collections written for this audience, it is important that they be made available for both private reading and shared experiences, so that more adolescents will have opportunities to meet poetry during these formative years. Much contemporary music has poetic quality and can be used as a springboard for exploring poems.

I LIKE YOU, IF YOU LIKE ME
compiled by Myra Cohn Livingston
Margaret K. McElderry Books, 1987
This anthology offers a selection of ninety poems by contemporary and traditional poets for all young people who explore the many aspects of friendship, from hilarious verses by X.J. Kennedy and Shel Silverstein to the poignant lines of Langston Hughes.

SEASON SONGS
Ted Hughes; ill. Leonard Baskin
Viking Press, 1975
Each of the four seasons are paid poetic tribute in selections written by Hughes.

SPACEWAYS
compiled by John Foster; ill. Allan Culless, Peter Elson, Alastair Graham, Tom Stimpson, Martin White
Oxford University Press, 1986
The world beyond our own planet is explored in this anthology of poems that paint pictures of the creatures, the skies, and the moons beyond Earth.

STRICTLY PRIVATE
edited by Roger McGough; ill. Graham Dean
Puffin, 1984
An anthology of modern poems selected by poet Roger McGough.

WORDS THAT TASTE GOOD
compiled by Bill Moore
Pembroke Publishers, 1987
More than 600 short, sparkling bits of poetry that will stir the imagination and stimulate interest in the power of words.

Index/Authors